Grace Sticks

JESUS IS THE WAY, THE TRUTH, AND THE LIFE

Grace Sticks

The Bumper Sticker Gospel for Restless Souls

KRISTINA ROBB-DOVER

With a foreword by
MICHAEL FROST

CASCADE *Books* · Eugene, Oregon

GRACE STICKS
The Bumper Sticker Gospel for Restless Souls

Copyright © 2013 Kristina Robb-Dover. All rights reserved. Except for brief quotations in critical publications or reviews, no part of this book may be reproduced in any manner without prior written permission from the publisher. Write: Permissions. Wipf and Stock Publishers, 199 W. 8th Ave., Suite 3, Eugene, OR 97401.

Unless otherwise noted, all biblical quotations are taken from the Holy Bible, New Revised Standard Version (NRSV), copyright © 1991, 1994 Oxford University Press, Inc.

Every effort has been made to obtain permissions for the bumper sticker images appearing in this work. If any required acknowledgments have been omitted, or any rights overlooked, it is unintentional. Please notify the publishers of any omission, and it will be rectified in future editions.

Cascade Books
An Imprint of Wipf and Stock Publishers
199 W. 8th Ave., Suite 3
Eugene, OR 97401

www.wipfandstock.com

ISBN 13: 978-1-62032-961-0

Cataloguing-in-Publication Data

Robb-Dover, Kristina.

    Grace sticks : the bumper sticker gospel for restless souls / Kristina Robb-Dover.

    X + Y p. ; 23 cm. Includes bibliographical references.

    ISBN 13: 978-1-62032-961-0

    1. Popular culture—Religious aspects. 2. Religion and culture—United States. I. Title.

BL65.C8 R4445 2013

Manufactured in the U.S.A.

*This book is for anyone anywhere who heard a version
of The Way, The Truth and The Life that made them feel more lost,
swindled or less alive—
and who made for the open road.*

*Nothing behind me, everything ahead of me,
as is ever on the road.*
—"Sal" in Jack Kerouac

*For faith is not the clinging to a shrine,
but an endless pilgrimage of the heart.*
—Abraham Heschel

Contents

Foreword by Michael Frost • ix
Preface • xiii
Aknowledgments • xv

1 Bumper Sticker Babylon:
   Our Babble, God's Gateway, or Both? • 1

The Way
2 "Don't Follow Me. I'm Lost Too!" • 15
3 "If You Can Read This, You Are Too Close." • 22
4 "Don't Let My Car Fool You. My Treasure Is in Heaven." • 33
5 "Honk If You Love Jesus. Text If You Want To Meet Him." • 42
6 "God Is My Co-Pilot" • 49

The Truth
7 "I've Got Nothing Against God,
   It's His Fan Club I Can't Stand." • 59
8 "Shit Happens" • 68
9 "True Love Waits" • 75
10 "The Next Time You Think You're Perfect,
    Try Walking on Water!!" • 81
11 "Visualize Whirled Peas" • 92

The Life

12 "Coexist" • 103
13 "He/She Who Dies with The Most Toys Wins." • 110
14 "Well Behaved Women Seldom Make History." • 116
15 "God Wants Spiritual Fruit, Not Religious Nuts" • 123
16 "got hope?" • 130

Foreword

I HAD KRISTINA ROBB-DOVER WRONG from the start. I had her pegged as the fair-haired girl of the Presbyterian set when I first met her at a conference for church leaders years ago—intelligent, articulate, conservative, churchy. Well, I was right about the first two, but after a Thai lunch in the Montrose near downtown Houston on a steamy summer's day, I changed my mind about the other two. Kristina was anything but conservative and churchy. She had an edgy sense of daring, like someone who knew how to balance on the cracks between contemporary secular culture and a quaint, old-fashioned church culture of respectability. She was hungry to discover more about how to be a faithful follower of the radical Jesus without having to fit into the bland, limp, unsavory straitjacket of a church that seems to be yearning to return to the days when "everyone" used to attend church and "Christian family values" reigned.

She reminded me of that generation of believers I had labeled "Exiles" and who I described in my book of the same name. I dedicated that book to folks just like Kristina even before I knew her when I wrote:

> This book is for those who can't remain in the safe modes of church and who wish to live expansive, confident Christian lives in this world without having to abandon themselves to the values of contemporary society. This book is for those Christians who feel themselves ready (or yearning) to jump ship but don't want to be left adrift in a world where greed, consumerism, laziness, and materialism toss them about endlessly and pointlessly. Such

Foreword

> Christians live with the nagging tension of being at home neither in the world nor in the church as they've known it.

Whenever I've seen her since (usually in pubs or bars, actually) and whenever I've read her blog *Fellowship of Saints and Sinners* I've had my initial suspicions about her shattered. She's a dweller on the threshold of a new way of doing and being the church. Frustrated with institutional religion, she is nonetheless expert at searching out God's grace in the most surprising places. As Alan Roxburgh once explained it, people like Kristina are building the bridge as they're walking on it.

From reading *Grace Sticks* I've come to realize that even though she occupies space in the liminal world between the church-as-it-was and the church-as-it's-becoming, she hasn't lost heart. She hasn't given in to cynicism or despair, something for which I'm very grateful. It excites me when I read her saying,

> If you are one of the many itinerant souls who has yet to arrive and for whom standing still is overrated, then this book is for you—because I suspect there really is as much grace to be had in the journeying itself as in the end destination.

Much grace to be had, indeed. This book is infused with grace. Sure, it offers incisive critiques here and there. It articulates frustration and annoyance at times. It yearns deeply for more and better ways of following Christ. And yet throughout it all is Kristina's winsome, sometimes quirky, always gracious voice lifting our gaze and reminding us of what's really important in the grand scheme of things. Who else but the most impassioned and gracious soul could write a book that quotes from Woody Allen, Anne Rice, Karl Barth, C. S. Lewis, Hadewijch of Antwerp, Louis CK, Rachel Held Evans, Ann Lamott, Jack Kerouac, and Wendell Berry? Grace bleeds through on every page, even when it comes from those surprising places.

It reminds me of Georges Bernanos's classic French novel, *Diary of a Country Priest*, which ends with the painful death from stomach cancer of the decent young curate—the country priest of the title. Through his difficult life, as recounted for us in his journal, he appears as a beacon of light in a dark and treacherous world. The church he serves has fallen into corruption and deceit. Bernanos, a devoted Christian, presents the good and honest young priest as a foil to the excesses of the church of his day. The other priests are self-absorbed and dreadfully flawed. Christ's reputation suffers at their hands. The young curate has served Christ faithfully, but now lies dying and we are forced to wonder at the harshness of his situation. He can no longer keep his diary. Another priest has been called to perform the last rites, but has not yet arrived. We discover the fate—and the wisdom—of the curate through a letter written by the friend who was with him at the very end:

> The priest was still on his way, and finally I was bound to voice my deep regret that such delay threatened to deprive my comrade of the final consolations of Our Church. He did not seem to hear me. But a few moments later he put his hand over mine, and his eyes entreated me to draw closer to him. He then uttered these words almost in my ear. And I am quite sure I have recorded them accurately, for his voice, though halting, was strangely distinct.
> "Does it matter? Grace is everywhere . . ."

Kristina's book is like the halting but distinct voice of the country priest. She loves the church too much to ignore its failings. She continues to hope for more. And yet this book is written with great compassion and empathy for the wandering soul, the disillusioned and the burnt out, the bothered and bewildered. It speaks to the spiritually vagrant and it promises the possibility of a place to call your spiritual home. Kristina Robb-Dover is wide-eyed and brutally frank about her misgivings with the traditional church, but she is also able to say gently but firmly, "Grace is everywhere. Grace sticks."

Michael Frost
Morling College
Sydney, Australia

Preface

Every year Spring announces her arrival in my city of Atlanta, Georgia with at least one reliable telltale sign: pollen. That yellow dust descends silently and intrepidly on cars, houses and streets, leaving a thin layer of nature's lint just about everywhere you look: car windshields; porch swings and patio furniture; bicyclists and their helmets; parents and their strollers. Pollen is all over the place.

Pollen finds its way through open windows, depositing itself on furniture, or lands on my shirt after a walk from the front door to the mailbox. Pollen sticks to my skin and hair, and gets into my nostrils and then my lungs, making me cough and wheeze. That is when I look frantically for the nasal spray from this time last year, then swear under my breath to discover the prescription ran out; or, when I remember why I am taking monthly allergy shots in the first place, and hope they prove their worth in all those trips to the clinic. Last year's pollen even stole my voice for a few days (maybe to the relief of my husband and kids); when I finally was able to be heard again, I sounded a bit like a chain-smoking version of the actress Debra Winger.

That sticky pollen is impossible to avoid: no matter how you might resist, it sneaks up on you and can be downright inconvenient. But it is also the sign that new life is just around the corner. Winter's last exhalations are giving way to the first blooms of azaleas and the flowering of dogwood trees, and the songs of the birds welcome the return of another spring.

Preface

If that pollen is irresistible and at times even painfully felt, it is also the prelude to a new beginning . . . a bit like grace. *Grace sticks, too.* So I have found to be true in my own life at least.

And, if this is where I, the author, tell you, the reader, why I am writing this book and why I am qualified to write it, then that admission pretty much says it all. Grace, unlike the migratory patterns of the Laysan Albatross, the lost art of coin making, or the endangered language of pidgin, requires no specialized education, expertise, or training. With God's grace, there are no qualifications: none of us measures up—and all of us are overly compensated, whether or not we know it.

"All is grace," said the late author Brennan Manning, who titled his final memoir with that declaration, and, from a survey of my own life, I concur. Grace can be sticky, annoying, and at times even painful; but it always signals a new beginning as reliably and miraculously as the annual visitation of Atlanta's magical fairy dust.

Grace has tenaciously stuck with me, in a way that only God can. Grace has clung to me when I could no longer hold on. Grace has picked me up when I have fallen. And, grace keeps telling me to keep putting one foot in front of the other—not merely for the sake of it, but because there are so many more scenic detours to make, homecomings to celebrate, and adventures to embark on.

This book represents my best effort at an introduction to that grace and to that God, and I am writing it for you. No matter where you are on your journey, I hope the words within these pages will remind you that just as grace is all around, so are the possibilities for new life and meaning and truth—all because of One who calls Himself The Way, The Truth, and The Life, and who invites us to come along and see for ourselves.

Acknowledgments

THIS BOOK HAS BEEN a work of love from start to finish, and I am not alone in having loved it into being.

Faithful friends and conversation partners have helped tell the story within these pages: Lara Catledge, Joan Gray, Megan Filston Johnson, Tammy Perlmutter, Anna Terry, Doug Webb, and Wendy Wyche have given me the courage to believe I had something to say and have offered helpful editorial feedback and/or invaluable moral support throughout the writing and revisions process. I cannot thank them enough.

Facebook friends and readers of my *Beliefnet* blog, "Fellowship of Saints and Sinners," have lent kind words of encouragement or insights along the way, some of which appear in the pages to come, and they, too, deserve a shout-out of appreciation. If it takes a village to raise a child, you have now convinced me that it takes a vigorous social platform to raise a book. I extend special thanks here to Jake Dell, Kate Nase McLean, Riley Powell, and Amy Richter for their periodic offers of help, advice or sheer encouragement.

Friends from the publishing world, Amy Frykholm and Richard Kauffman (*The Christian Century*), Len Goss (formerly with Zondervan), Rob Kerby and the staff of *Beliefnet*, Therese Neumann (Penguin), Jana Riess (author of *Flunking Sainthood*), Dave Schroeder (The A Group), and most especially, my able editor Rodney Clapp and the dedicated people of Wipf and Stock Publishers, have all contributed either to the development and publication of *Grace Sticks*, or the grit to keep writing it, or both. To you I am indebted.

Acknowledgments

An affectionate "thank you" also goes to Joe's Coffee in East Atlanta—for the bottomless mugs of coffee and the endearingly quirky company, which made an otherwise solitary exercise fun on the good days and tolerable on the bad ones—and to the men and women of The Monastery of the Holy Spirit, for opening your home as a place for retreat and inspiration.

"Mama Susan" and the widows and orphans of Amazing Grace Orphanage, in Adjumani, northern Uganda, you never cease to inspire me, and I cannot thank you enough for putting one foot in front of the other in one of the most trying places on God's earth, and then letting me walk alongside you in that journey.

I'm grateful to my parents, John and Lori Robb, who introduced me to Jesus at an early age and have lived their lives as if The Way, The Truth and The Life really were the only thing that mattered—so much so that, fittingly, one of their cars sports a bumper sticker that reads "Jesus is The Way, The Truth and The Life."

I also owe oodles of thanks to my devoted husband, Paul Dover, who by the time of publication will have braved more than a year's worth of Saturdays as a single dad in order to help me write this book, and who was also the first courageous soul to read a very rough manuscript and lend his able editing tips and contributions. My children, Cam and Sam, who put up with their mother's absences with a disappointingly low level of protest, also deserve thanks.

The eclectic strains of theologians and thinkers both past and present can be discerned within the pages that follow, either in the form of direct quotations and paraphrases or as subtler but still influential cadences. These inform a work that, while defying categorization, might best be described as a deeply personal, unsystematic theological travel guide for restless souls, one that is both confessional and postmodern. Augustine, Hans Urs Von Balthasar, Karl Barth, Amy Julia Becker, Rob Bell, Ellen Charry, Wendy Farley, Michael Frost, Rachel Held-Evans, Alan Hirsch, Anne Lamott, Brennan Manning, Tom Long, Jürgen Moltmann, Henri Nouwen, Gregory of Nyssa, Dorothy Sayers, Friedrich Schleiermacher, A. J. Swoboda, and Barbara Brown Taylor comprise this diverse crew of pastors, thinkers, missiologists and writers, whose contributions to my spiritual and intellectual journey cannot go without mention.

Acknowledgments

A special note of thanks here goes to friend Michael Frost, whose regularly bold challenges to the church to be a people formed by the heart of God also make him a role model: thank you for your foreword and more importantly for your ministry.

Finally, and before these acknowledgements become indistinguishable from the gushing ramblings of a first-time Oscar winner, I'm thankful to God for this crazy idea and for sustaining me in those darker moments of writer's block and existential worry. You are both the Source and Consummation of this restless soul's wanderlust, and for that, I give You thanks and praise. To You alone be every bead of sweat, fit of tears, sleepless night, peal of laughter, and humorous or heartbreaking confession that forms the story line within these pages and makes my journey so wondrously incomplete. Amen.

1

Bumper Sticker Babylon
Our Babble, God's Gateway, or Both?

> *By the rivers of Babylon we sat and wept when we remembered Zion.*
> —PSALM 137:1

> *The day of my spiritual awakening was the day I saw—and knew I saw—all things in God and God in all things.*
> —MECHTILD OF MAGDEBURG

THIS IS THE FIRST of my confessions: I've never put a bumper sticker on my car. The only time I came close was when a certain politician was running for office, and even then it was only by proxy that I joined the ranks of the many Americans who choose to wear their views on their cars in lieu of their sleeves. My husband put the sticker on his bumper, with the result that I, a church pastor at the time, chose to drive our other unclothed vehicle to work.

Grace Sticks

Still, while I have yet to summon up enough courage to become the vehicular poster girl for the next worthy cause or passionately held belief, I have harbored a curiosity about—and even a shy admiration for—those who make their rear bumpers moving billboards. You might even say that I have cultivated a hobby out of reading these slogans above other people's tailpipes. The 1969 Volkswagen perched in the parking lot, "scattered, smothered and covered" in full-blown, Waffle House style, like some postmodern totem pole in homage to its artist. Or the soccer parent's Honda Odyssey with the one token, silver fish emblem, encircling the word, "Jesus" (or, if not Jesus, then "Darwin"). Or the Chevrolet with the cryptic saying that you struggle to make sense of and are still decoding the next day.

Amusingly, while it is considered gauche to talk about politics or religion around the dinner table or in polite company, many of us have found therapeutic outlets for self-expression about these very same things on our back bumpers. Pithy aphorisms. Funny quotations. Senseless double entèndres. In-your-face declarations of what we believe. Our bumper stickers are an open, sometimes voyeuristic window onto our hearts and the things that inspire, offend, infuriate, move, embarrass, and perplex us.

In my line of work, I spend a whole lot of time in the car. These comings and goings are often marked by the mindless entertainment of bumper stickers, be they idling at a light or lounging in a parking lot. Bumper stickers often catch my attention and frequently elicit at least a laugh or a pair of raised eyebrows, if not an exclamation of disbelief.

There are also the times when bumper stickers signify more than mere amusement, insofar as they imply something about their owner: for example, that bumper sticker on the luxury SUV, recklessly weaving through traffic at seventy-miles-per-hour on the freeway, which reads, "My tapeworm is smarter than your honor student"; or the dilapidated pickup truck, overladen by second-hand furniture threatening to topple at any moment, which sports the rear-end declaration, "I'm just here to annoy you."

I have encountered many a self-revelation by a stranger with the help of only a few sound bites on their car. Maybe you have, too.

Like those two telling stickers a friend recently spied on somebody's truck: the first read, "I thought I met my knight in shining armor, but he turned out to be a dork in tin foil"; the second, "So Many 2x4's So Few Studs."

A bumper sticker, however silly, stupid or offensive, can offer a glimpse into the aspirations of the driver. What are they seeking or not seeking? To what do they give pride of place? In what do they derive their sense of purpose? In this way, a short caption over a tailpipe can speak beyond itself. Your bumper stickers tell me something about who you are, where you come from and what you believe or long for; as nuggets of meaning, truth or life in a changing world, they can help narrate an ever-evolving story.

In a similar manner, then, the bumper stickers within these pages navigate my own, unique itinerary of grace. They best encapsulate how a gracious God has become real to me in all my wonderings and wanderings. They are signposts on my journey.

But these God sightings are yours also. They are yours because I have read them on the back of your Subaru station wagon or Ford Escort, or because you, too, have been entertained by their silliness while fumbling for your keys in the parking lot or sitting at an interminably long red light. They are yours in that you, too, have found them funny, inspirational, stupid, or infuriating. They are yours if you really do "honk if you love Jesus" and "text if you want to meet Him."

IN RESTLESS PURSUIT OF MORE

If bumper stickers provide a fun, familiar currency in which to swap stories and reflections at the intersection between life and God, they also uncover the "More" we have yet to find in our spiritual journeys.[1] As distinctively American artifacts, they can embody

---

1. "The More" is an expression first borrowed from Barbara Brown Taylor: "It may be the name for a longing—for more meaning, more feeling, more connection, more life," she writes. See Taylor, *An Altar in the World*, xiii-xiv. Similarly, throughout his memoir *All Is Grace*, Brennan Manning employs the expression ("more") to talk about his own spiritual journey. See Manning, *All Is Grace*, 88, 91, etc.

(if imperfectly) the increasingly pervasive spiritual restlessness of our time.[2] These days a growing number of these souls are leaving church and not looking back, or seeking something more than what they discovered there. They, to quote the words of the band U2, "still haven't found what [they're] looking for."[3]

A poll released in October 2012 by the Pew Forum on Religion and Public Life found one in five Americans and one out of three adults under the age of thirty now describes himself as either "spiritual but not religious" or "neither spiritual nor religious."[4] These "Nones" are generally between the ages of eighteen and sixty-four, and their number is steadily rising.[5] If they are not all young in years, these restless souls are young in spirit: they eschew easy answers for the adventure of living the questions; they shun hypocrisy and long for an experience of what is real and true over neatly packaged doctrines; they are distrustful of organized religion and its traditional authority figures; they prefer the freedom of the open road to any religious collective, which, with appeals to money, power, and institutional preservation, would seek to bind their souls.

My own experience is that you do not have to be religiously unaffiliated to be a restless soul. Restless souls are *in* churches, too, if not as members then as regular attenders. In fact I would venture to guess there are many of us who, despite attending church worship services at least occasionally, find ourselves on the margins of the church, or reluctant to join the church for some of the same reasons cited by the religiously unaffiliated.

Whether churched or unchurched, religious or non-religious, we are restless souls because we seek "the More" we have yet to find in our churches.

2. For a discussion of the quintessentially American manifestations of this "spiritual restlessness," see Leigh Eric Schmidt, *Restless Souls: The Making of American Spirituality*. I derive my use of the expression "restless souls" from Schmidt; the sense in which I employ the term will both overlap and differ from Schmidt's.

3. U2, "I Still Haven't Found What I'm Looking For," *The Joshua Tree*.

4. Stencel et al., "'Nones' on the Rise: One-in-Five Adults Have No Religious Association," para. 8.

5. See chart titled "Demographic Profile" in ibid.

More meaning and direction.
More honest-to-God truth.
More fullness of life.

Whether or not we call ourselves Christian, many of us have found ourselves in existential exile looking for answers. We have paused to bemoan in our times the almost paralyzing confusion wrought by an endless menu of spiritual entrées; and, we have grieved when our noblest religious pursuits or best self-help strategies have let us down. We know there is More and are somewhere on a quest to find It, but have grown a bit dejected in the process.

Some of us have seen our idealism about the church go up in smoke after having been wounded by the very institution in which we hoped to taste and see God's goodness—but instead found condemnation and hypocrisy.[6] Others of us have grown weary with the petty, self-absorbed political squabbles that besiege our denominations and churches, calling into question truths we had thought were fundamental to Christianity, like forgiveness and the love of neighbor. Many of us hoped to find spiritual refuge and belonging only to discover the institutional church was no different from the rest of the world—just another dangerous, cynical, power-hungry bunch of people bedeviled by the same demons that plague everyone else. Like the writer Anne Rice, who converted to Christianity only to reject it soon after because of disillusionment with the church, we have left and not looked back, our spiritual taste buds turned off by what we found there.

Then there are those of us who have searched high and low to find spiritual belonging elsewhere with differing levels of success. We have thrown ourselves into one pursuit after another, from meditation to yoga to psychotherapy, all in hopes of finding our spiritual place in the universe. We wander here and there across barren religious plains looking for a shelter that we can genuinely call "home."

And, if many of us have wandered far from where we first set out, our bumper stickers are like the trinkets or memorabilia we collect along the way. Sometimes, like children walking on a beach,

---

6. Psalm 34:8.

we become so distracted by the uniqueness of a particular shell—be it the teachings of the Dalai Lama or the self-help optimism of a Joel Osteen—that we stop to notice it, then slip it in our pocket. We may admire its beauty. Or laugh at its eccentricity. Or wonder at its meaning. Or nod firmly in agreement. We may not even know why these shells in particular glimmer—just that they do enough for us to hold on to them; and in this way we can meander from one god, attachment, longing, or conviction, to another.

If our souls are restless, our lives are in constant flux, too. We are constantly coming and going or arriving only to leave—not just in and out of churches, but in and out of jobs, or in and out of relationships. In this great river of change, our individual lives and all they contain—our finances, health, or love interests—can appear as little more than swift-moving currents.

Various dimensions of our shared human experience serve only to feed this existential restiveness. The breakneck speed of social networking and information technologies. The vicarious interconnectedness of stock markets. The insecurity of a rapidly changing job market. A delicate web of global relationships. The breakdown of traditional family structures. We are like fast-paced atoms forever bumping up against one another and changing in the process. It is exhausting just to think about!

What rest, then, if any really, might we find in bumper stickers? Maybe more than we would be inclined to think.

These quirky, sometimes outlandish displays of our various attachments have often been dismissed as mere spiritual window dressing—symbols of the shallow, vacuous nature of contemporary spirituality. The epithet "bumper sticker Christianity" has been intoned disparagingly, for example, as a way to describe the often superficial, consumerist-driven, culture-warring, politicized nature of the church in America.[7] Centuries after their forebears

---

7. For example, Tim Tennent writes: "Evangelicals have become experts in finding a thousand new ways to ask the same question, '*What is the* **least** *one has to do to become a Christian.*' That's our defining question. We've become masters at theological and soteriological minimalism. We are the ones who have boiled the entire glorious Gospel down to a single phrase, a simple emotive transaction, or some silly slogan. It is time for a new generation of Christians, committed to apostolic faith, to declare this minimalistic, reductionistic

died at the stakes or in the gladiatorial ring for their testimonies to the resurrected Jesus, and when today many around the world still face persecution for their faith, many who self-identify as Christian would protest the notion that our witness to Christ could or should be reduced to a few catchy sound bites on the back of a car.

This is understandable. It is especially understandable if the messages we promote on our vehicles really are nothing more than our narcissistic indulgence in self-expression, and as such mere babble.

But if bumper stickers are this, are they this only? Could it be that in a sea of endless ripples, waves and permutations, bumper stickers are like small islands of meaning? Is it possible that these peel-and-stick messages unwittingly pay homage to the More that we long for and catch only fleeting glimpses of? Might they, by setting apart and remembering something that we have come to know and love or learn from, point to the God we worship unknowingly?[8] What if bumper stickers, in all their frivolity, were really pointing us to the One who calls Himself "the Way, the Truth and the Life"?

GRACE IN A COMMON TONGUE

The country of Babylon in the time of ancient Israel was an exotic, uninviting place where the exiled Hebrew people, having been crushed into service by their Babylonian conquerors, were at drift

---

Christianity a failed project!" See Tennent, "Bumper Sticker Christianity," para. 3.

8. A biblical parallel would be the first-century Grecian shrines to which the apostle Paul refers in his speech to the people of Athens. See Acts 17:22–28: "Then Paul stood in front of the Areopagus and said, 'Athenians, I see how extremely religious you are in every way. For as I went through the city and looked carefully at the objects of your worship, I found among them an altar with the inscription, *To an unknown god*. What therefore you worship as unknown, this I proclaim to you. The God who made the world and everything in it, he who is Lord of heaven and earth, does not live in shrines made by human hands, nor is he served by human hands, as though he needed anything, since he himself gives to all mortals life and breath and all things . . . For *in him we live and move and have our being*; as even some of your own poets have said, *For we too are his offspring*.'"

in a sea of many gods. They found themselves pining away for a bygone age when faith was simpler, God was One and the Word of God really meant something—and not just to senile grandmothers. They longed for a time when God, as the One in whom they lived, moved and had their being, was all in all. They looked and waited for a day when they would no longer have to search vainly for God's presence but might experience God directly in their very midst.

I suspect many of us have shared similar laments and longings that spring out of the times in which we live. We may not have thrown ourselves down in anguish at the rivers of Babylon and wept when we remembered our lost Zion—but we may have shaken our heads at the depressing state of mainstream Christianity in America, choosing instead to spend our Sunday mornings at the local farmers' market or with a newspaper at a coffee shop. We may have wandered far from where we first began only to discover we now have no spiritual bed on which to lie.[9] In a desolate land of many options, many of them disappointing, we can feel existentially empty and alone, grieving what we have lost while knowing full well we cannot return to it. You might say, then, that in this sense many of us in twenty-first-century America live in Babylon, too—only our Babylon might be summed up in bumper stickers.

"Babylon" in its original usage had two meanings: it meant both "babble" and "gateway to God." If Babylon signified Israel's place of existential meaninglessness—the seemingly unredeemable "gibberish" in Israel's story—Babylon was also where the one true God would show up for His people. Babylon was where Israel's dead-end would become God's avenue of redemption and where Israel's blather would hasten an encounter with the Living God.

Maybe something similar could be said about bumper stickers. Sometimes our babble can be the very place where God meets us. Sometimes our mumbo jumbo, whether or not we know it, is like a big "SOS" sign for grace to find us.

And, if bumper stickers are mostly skin-deep vestiges of meaning in an existentially barren landscape, they can also point us to God, serving as a conduit to the Holy even as they assault

---

9. The allusion is to Jesus's words in Luke 9:58: "Foxes have holes, and birds of the air have nests; but the Son of Man has nowhere to lay his head."

our senses. In the same moment that they pay lip service to the things we hold dear, they can shine a light on our souls, illuminating the goodness there and beckoning us back to the ultimate Goodness which is the Source of all good. If bumper stickers are stupid, frivolous, preposterous, or revolting—if they're little more than our own silly, commodified gibberish—they still may knowingly or unknowingly welcome a visitation from the One who made us and will never let us go. (The door mats on the front steps of our souls are rarely suitable for visitors, after all; but I'm convinced God still shows up there, brushing off the feet, then knocking to see if anyone is home.[10] Our bumper stickers are a bit like those welcome mats, whether or not we were expecting guests.)

This book, then, is based on the novel premise that bumper stickers can be both our babble and a place of encounter with the grace of God.

I would like to think in fact that bumper stickers, as a rare combination of the sacred and the mundane, can serve as popular "sacraments" of sorts. "Sacraments" in that they mediate God's grace in and through some of the most accessible objects in our postmodern, American context. Bumper stickers are sacred because they say something about the values we hold dear and the goods we desire (or, inversely, the evils we decry); but they are also mundane because we can encounter them just about anywhere we look. We don't have to step into a Buddhist temple or a Catholic monastery to find them. We don't have to speak a particular religious language or follow certain liturgical cues to interpret them. They are just there. Often right in front of us. On the highway, with the windows down and the wind blowing through our hair, or in bumper-to-bumper traffic. At the light waiting to turn green. In the mall parking lot. They are just there—everywhere—holding out a particular way, truth, or life, and giving voice often unknowingly to our aspirations for the Way, the Truth, and the Life.

With respect to this quintessentially American sacrament, then, it would seem that we remain incurably religious. If today we

---

10. "Listen! I am standing at the door, knocking; if you hear my voice and open the door, I will come in to you and eat with you, and you with me," Jesus says in Revelation 3:20.

Grace Sticks

Americans are less likely to associate with any one denomination or religious group, or to attend any one church or house of worship, we continue to dress up our cars with the zeal of new converts.[11] If today we flit from one church or house of worship to another like whimsical consumers in a newly dynamic spiritual marketplace, we are still often loyal, at least unconsciously, to our bumper stickers.[12] Even the most humorous or flippant declarations on our back bumpers set us apart in some way. They announce our tribal affiliation.

And these peel-and-stick messages seem to last long after we have left church or lost our religion. The laminated "Coexist" mandate that your partner attached to your jeep years ago? I venture to guess that it is still there, having survived even your most adventurous off-roading detours in the Alaskan wilderness. (Maybe it even made it through the ensuing break-up with your partner five years later.) The "Got Hope?" sticker that in a fit of inspiration you sealed to your back fender? It is still probably there, too, testifying to more than just unwavering loyalty to your favorite presidential candidate.[13]

This all begs a question: what if we actually *talked* about how bumper stickers gesture in some way or another to the More we seek? More direction. More truth. More life.

What if these sometimes pithy, sometimes ridiculous statements became touchstones for a conversation about God, life, and the stuff innbetween—a conversation not just for traditional, so-called church folk, or for the "spiritual but not religious," but for all restless souls, whether in the church or out. This book belongs to that conversation. A conversation about at least some of the things we hold most dear, or find most appalling, or question or doubt, as well as a shared language in which to talk about these things—all

---

11. Regarding Americans' itinerant, "pick-and-choose" religious habits, see Lugo et al., "U.S. Religious Landscape Survey," para. 9. Carol Gardner has concluded from extensive research and travel all around the country that Americans are faithfully wedded to their bumper stickers. See Gardner, *Bumper Sticker Wisdom: America's Pulpit Above the Tailpipe*, 8.

12. Gardner, *Bumper Sticker Wisdom*, 6–7.

13. Laziness (being too apathetic to remove that sticker) might be another explanation for why our bumper stickers have such staying adhesive power, but I'm guessing that laziness is not a good enough explanation here.

with a view to encountering more meaning, more truth and more life (in essence, grace) and the God who wants to give us these things.[14]

For the many of us who find church lingo and God talk off-putting or intimidating, I hope the bumper stickers within these pages will spark the kind of invitational conversation you might find over a beer with your local bartender or at a coffee shop with a good friend. Gritty honesty. Non-judgmental listening. Therapeutic laughter. Maybe a good cry here or there. The clinking of glasses. Hopefully, more laughter.

So this conversation is yours as much as it is mine: it is yours if you as a fellow traveler on life's open road have ever wandered far from home and felt lost or free or both at the same time; or are still wondering and wandering and restlessly seeking on a quest for More.

If you are one of the many itinerant souls who has yet to arrive and for whom standing still is overrated, then this book is for you—because I suspect there really is as much grace to be had in the journeying itself as in the end destination.

You may read the enclosed messages differently, or they may lead you down other paths to gaze at other views. But in the end, I would like to think that if my own experience of trying on bumper stickers for size helps you see God just a bit better in your own restless comings and goings, and to meet God there, then this book will have succeeded in drawing both of us closer to the One in whom all our journeys begin and end. Because if Jesus really is who he says he is— if Jesus is "the Way, the Truth, and the Life"—then all of our comings and goings, wanderings and standing stills, seeking and finding, and all of the various signposts that direct us here, there and everywhere, ultimately find their place in Christ. In his life, death and resurrection. In his Story—apart from which I am inclined to think it really is all just babble.

---

14. In this most religiously pluralistic period of our nation's history, when traditional religious symbols and terms have become at best irrelevant and at worst offensive and alienating to broad segments of our population, bumper stickers may spark a more light-hearted dialogue about what gives us meaning, truth, or life, and about the Giver of these things.

The Way

Jesus answered, "I am the Way..."
JOHN 14:6

2

DON'T FOLLOW ME — I'M LOST, TOO!

> *Be like the fox who makes more tracks than necessary, some in the wrong direction.*
> —Wendell Berry

> *Lord I don't know which way I am going . . . Still got such a long way to go.*
> —Coldplay

John Lennon once said that, "life is what happens to you while you're busy making other plans."[1]

---

1. John Lennon, "Beautiful Boy," *Double Fantasy*.

The Way

I guess getting lost is a bit like that, too: when you are on your way somewhere, you can find yourself unexpectedly nowhere, or at least in the last place you would have wanted to be; when you are busy heading in one direction, you can find yourself having to take a U-turn or following the "detour" signs or stopping at a Mini Mart to ask the clueless cashier for help; and then you can find yourself in the wrong place at the wrong time.

That was how it was for me one night returning from my high school prom. My date had showed up proudly in his parents' Acura; we had then exchanged corsages and endured a round of awkward picture-taking before we set off for a hotel in Los Angeles for an evening of chaperoned dinner and dancing. Before that, I had spent the day absorbed in teenaged self-beautification, at the Macy's cosmetics counter for a free makeover and sunbathing in our backyard, obsessively working on my tan lines in order to wear a strapless blue dress.

The year was 1991, and that blue-sequined, velvet dress with the very large, satin, bouffant bow was evidence that the fashion of the eighties was still alive and well.

The night would have passed relatively uneventfully. (My date was shy enough not to try kissing me—and while he was a nice guy, I was kind of relieved; the only real drama at the party had been one girl fainting because her dress was too tight.)

We soon found ourselves back in the car headed for home with only one stop to make—a gas station.

We didn't know our whereabouts; we had wandered around on surface streets not far from the hotel; but we figured any gas station would do. When we pulled into one, we didn't even notice the cops at first, or the fact that the red lights on their cars were silently flashing. It took a policeman walking over to my date, now standing at the pump, to help us understand where we were and why we needed to leave in a jiffy: apparently we had just pulled into the scene of a shoot-out only minutes earlier, and the suspect was still on the loose. We would have to fill up our gas tank somewhere else.

I remember thinking in those few short moments as my date hastily turned on the ignition and we sped out of there that I would have preferred to be just about anywhere else. Even if *anywhere* was pre-calculus class, taught in the thick German accent of a pedantic Mr. Bruchner (or was it Buchner?), *anywhere* would be better than where I was. Anywhere other than a random gas station in some seedy borough of downtown L.A.

We were lost, so you might imagine our relief when we found our way back to the freeway headed in the direction of home. Never before had my soullessly suburban, Southern Californian neighborhood looked so good.

LOST: THE REALITY VERSION

It doesn't take mistakenly finding oneself at the scene of a shoot-out to feel vulnerable, out of place, and confused about how one got there. I suspect that most of us in any manner of ways have felt like this before. We all get lost at one point or another, some of us more than others. We start out married and end up divorced. We land a dream job only to lose it. We do our best to stay healthy and wind up with cancer. We embark on life young, idealistic, and sure about who we are, only to discover years later that we are not the person we thought we were and that the person we are today we do not even recognize.

And then there are the ways that we can be lost and not even know it. We might join a church and adopt the lingo. We might pray regularly and tithe ten percent. We might even use our Bibles like built-in GPS systems for navigating life's twists and turns—so much so that we say with certainty, to quote another bumper sticker, "I found it."

All the while on the inside we can be like the "white-washed tombs" Jesus rebukes.[2] (Jesus, after all, saves his harshest words for the folks who are convinced they have found the way and have all the answers.) Every sure-sounding answer for every doubt-filled question can be little more than a coping mechanism—a way to

---

2. Matthew 23:27–28.

paper over our deepest inner fears and anxieties—when in fact we wear a veil of self-deception that keeps us from looking squarely in the face of life's complexities and grieving our own incapacity to make sense of them.

Jesus calls this sort of thing "blindness." And we are all probably blind in one way or another. Being blind is not only part of what it means to be lost; it is also part of what it means to be human. But most of us first need to feel the ground underneath our feet shake in order for that veil of self-deception to tear and come apart at the seams. Sometimes it takes the death of a child, or hitting rock bottom because of an addiction, or the Twin Towers of the World Trade Center crumbling, to wrench us free of these cheap plastic-imitation answers.

In the movie *Higher Ground*, director and actor Vera Farmiga's character, Corinne Walker, is a young woman struggling to live out her Christian walk. When a dear friend's surgery for a brain tumor confines her once lively and sensuous friend to a vegetative state and life in a wheelchair, Corinne begins to wrestle with doubt. She begins to question the sunny, unruffled certainty of her pastor and fellow believers' trust in God's good purposes. Corinne then begins to question all that she has become, including her role as a dutiful, Christian wife. When she and her husband visit a Christian marriage therapist, she is told she must either repent in order to save her marriage or face eternal damnation in hell. Corinne's inability to sit easily with such cut-and-dry answers eventually leads her to an uneasy acceptance: she acknowledges that her faith is real to the degree that it is doubt-filled, and that she sees God only insofar as she acknowledges the limitations of her vision.

But it takes a crisis to thrust Corinne out of the self-deception that she has "found it."[3] Like Corinne, many of us who claim to have found it can convince ourselves that it is our job to dispense directions, so that faith is a road map of sorts for how to live, and we, the local AAA office passing out free road maps to passersby.

---

3. The expression "found it" comes from the bumper sticker that reads, "I found it."

The problem, though, is that faith is not ours to give in the first place. The Bible calls faith "a gift from God."[4]

Nor is faith a map to keep us from losing our way.

The reality is that God's people are always getting lost—not just once but over and over again. Moses and the people of Israel spend more than forty years wandering around aimlessly in the wilderness before they enter the Promised Land. The crowds following Jesus are at times "like sheep without a shepherd," so much so that they invoke Jesus's pity; and even Jesus's disciples regularly betray how clueless they are when it comes to what God is up to.[5]

If there were one person in scripture about whom it legitimately could be said that he "found it," it would be the Apostle Paul. But consider for a moment how Paul finds Jesus. God appears to Paul on the road to Damascus in a vision so blinding that Paul is unable to see for three days.[6] This is the God whose name is so holy it cannot be pronounced, so that the Jewish people in their Scriptures choose to render it by the consonants "YHWH." The sign that Paul has met this God is Paul's ensuing blindness.

Which makes me wonder if when we think we have found God once and for all, we have really found something else—something other than God, that is. Because God can't be found on our terms or with the maps we draw. *God finds us.* And we will know when God finds us because the experience will only reiterate just how truly lost and blind we have been all along.

This I think is the paradox of God's grace, and it explains how one who claims to have seen Jesus in the flesh can exclaim that he is "chief" among sinners.[7] We are found only insofar as we acknowledge our lostness. We catch "glimpses" of God only to the degree that we recognize our blindness.

---

4. Ephesians 2:8.
5. Matthew 9:36.
6. Acts 9:3–9.
7. 1 Timothy 1:15.

LOST AND FOUND

If much of scripture is about lost people, it is also about lost people being found.

Jesus says that he came "to seek and save the lost," and scripture affirms that God "does some of God's best work with people who are truly, seriously lost," as Barbara Brown Taylor puts it.[8]

The fact is that God doesn't seem to have much time for those who don't know they're lost. Consider the story Jesus tells in Luke 18, which goes something like this: there is a minister who has followed the Good Book all her life, so much so that she teaches others how to be good Christians; she is convinced that she is on the right path, so much so that one day, hearing all of the news about greedy Wall Street traders who have blown tax payer money on big bonuses, she thanks God that she is not like these Wall Street traders who have lost their way, and she recounts all of the ways in which she has modeled a holy life. She has tithed ten percent. She serves in the soup kitchen and goes on mission trips each year. She even makes guest appearances in the children's nursery on some Sunday mornings.

But the Wall Street trader with the big bonus sees the error in his ways. He gets down on his knees and with tears running down his cheeks, prays for God's forgiveness and mercy.

"Which of these two is justified?" Jesus asks. Which of these two is now in right relationship with their Creator?

You guessed it.

God is on a mission to find lost people and redeem the dead ends, detours, and U-turns of our lives. There is something, therefore, enormously freeing and powerfully transformative about being lost—precisely because it forces us to fall back against our own incapacity to find our way apart from God's grace alone. When we lose our jobs or ruin our marriages, or become chronically sick or suffer the loss of a loved one, it can feel like the bottom of our world has fallen out. So we cuss at the map we were holding. Or, we hold on to our seats for dear life. Or, we find ourselves flat on our backs with the wind knocked out of us. But it is in times like these when friends desert us that we discover who our true friends are; and

---

8. Taylor, *An Altar in the World*, 73.

when we give up on God that God reaches out to us; and when despair is our only companion that hope tiptoes in through the door that we slammed in its face. And in this process of waking up to the reality of our lostness we are found.

The beautiful thing is that when we are most lost we are also closest to God's heart. That is when God comes looking for us, like the "Good Shepherd" who lays down his life for the lost sheep.[9] I have learned in my own life that God does this not just once but over and over again. God comes looking for me when I, like a thick-skulled sheep, lose my way.

And it seems to me that being a Christian means being above all else brutally honest about the fact that we really don't have the directions ourselves. And that we're not the ones to follow. And that while we all along have been getting lost, there has been Somebody there finding us over and over again—and that Somebody is the Way.

DISCUSSION QUESTIONS

1. *Have you seen this bumper sticker before? If so, how did you interpret it? Do you agree or disagree with Kristina's interpretation of it?*

2. *Have you seen the bumper sticker, "I found it"? What do you think it means? Do you think Christians are people who have found it? Why, and in what sense . . . or, why not?*

3. *Can you recall a time when you were physically or existentially lost? What was it like? What did you learn from the experience? How did the experience change you?*

4. *What are the ways that we can be blind and/or lost?*

5. *What stories from scripture come to mind when you reflect on what it means to be lost and/or blind and God's response?*

6. *How do you react to the idea that Christian identity means not giving directions but admitting that we are lost and found, sometimes over and over again? Do you agree or disagree?*

---

9. John 10:11.

3

**IF YOU CAN READ THIS...
YOU ARE
TOO CLOSE!**

And this is one of the major questions of our lives: how we keep boundaries, what permission we have to cross boundaries, and how we do so.
—A.B. Yehoshua

Your sacred space is where you can find yourself again and again.
—Joseph Campbell

THERE ARE FEW THINGS more annoying than being tailgated. You know what I'm talking about.

The huge SUV with the obnoxiously bright headlights that flash in your rear windshield mirror when you're already driving above the speed limit.

On the highway.

In pouring rain.

With little children in the back seat.

It is in moments like these that, with one quick flip of the "tall man," I am most in danger of losing my Christian witness . . .

Until I find myself running late one day, my foot heavy on the accelerator, when a sweet, elderly couple with out-of-state plates pulls out in front of me, chugging along at an achingly slow twenty-five mph in a thirty-five mph speed zone.

They are enjoying the sights of downtown Atlanta as if they are on a safari tour through the grasslands of Kenya.

They have no clue that the driver behind them is about to be fined for arriving ten minutes late to pick up her child from day care.

Once, I pulled up close enough to be able to catch through his side-view mirror Gramps' bifocals and his geriatric gaze, thinking to myself, "Should you still be licensed to drive, Mister?"

I sidled up so close that I could see him frowning through his rear-view mirror, because I was *too close.*

He kept on puttering along at a snail's pace, anyway.

BOUNDARIES AS SELF-PRESERVATION

Boundaries are a funny thing. We human beings seem both to need them and to rebel against them. In the very beginning, the Bible says that God places a tree in the middle of the Garden of Eden and tells the man and the woman not to eat from it. And I wonder if a sign that read, "If you can read this, you are too close," might have helped—because the man and the woman trespass. They cross the boundary in spite of God's command. They eat from the tree of the knowledge of good and evil and find themselves in a desolate place where they now must live with the consequences of their trespass.

The Way

We all need boundaries. They are there for our own good. Boundaries help us live safely and are a source of freedom even as they place limits on us.

God in scripture gives the Ten Commandments to the people of Israel, but why?[1] Is it so God can shake God's finger at them like an officious school marm or ruthless parking lot attendant, reminding them that God is watching to see when they will next slip up or park in the wrong space? Is it so God can keep some heavenly ledger that tallies up all of the ways that we fall short, and then present it to us one day when we reach the gates of paradise? I don't think so. I suspect it is really because God, like any loving parent, wants the best for his children and knows they can benefit from some basic parameters about how to live in relation to their Maker and to one another.

And do we succeed in keeping all of the commandments ever, really? Of course not! The results can be devastating.

A friend overheard an especially memorable conversation over lunch that she later shared on Facebook.

"Hi, nice to meet you," the conversation began. "I'm not sure how to start this conversation. I guess . . . how long have you been sleeping with my boyfriend?"

This bizarre introduction apparently preceded, according to my friend's description, "a twenty-minute discussion at very high volume on details of the past few months (who was with him at what time, how he was found out, sharing of texts/photos/love notes/etc)." Then, as if the encounter could not become any weirder, the two women exchanged a "cordial handshake," left, and the entire café "erupted in laughter."

---

1. The Ten Commandments (in Exodus 20) comprise the following exhortations, purported to have been issued to Moses by God himself: "you shall have no other gods before me"; "you shall not make for yourself an idol"; "you shall not make wrongful use of the Lord your God"; "remember the Sabbath day, and keep it holy"; "honor your father and mother"; "you shall not murder"; "you shall not commit adultery"; "you shall not steal"; "you shall not bear false witness against your neighbor"; and, "you shall not covet your neighbor's house . . . wife . . . slave . . . ox . . . donkey . . . or anything that belongs to your neighbor."

My friend's conclusion: "We live in a very strange world sometimes."[2]

Strange, yes, but maybe not altogether unexplainable. Because if God's commands are there to gesture to God's best for us, God out of love also gives us the freedom to flout these rules or flat-out ignore them and face the consequences. Sometimes we will miss the "Warning: Keep Out" sign, having not really seen the words, "you shall have no other gods before me"; other times we will flagrantly plow through the barricade, having seen from far away in bold, "Don't Covet," in front of another's money, possessions or spouse, but plowing full steam ahead, anyway. That is when we can find ourselves doing the equivalent of making awkward introductions to strangers in cafés.

C. S. Lewis, in describing the garden variety capacity of human beings to trespass and, in turn, wreak havoc, puts it this way: "We are not merely imperfect creatures that need to grow, but also rebels who need to lay down our arms."[3]

Maybe God gives us boundaries so that we don't have to take up arms in a battle we are bound to lose.

BOUNDARIES AS SELF-FORMATION

When they were around two, both of my children almost overnight morphed from sweet, smiley little angels into practiced little rebels without causes. They quickly took to throwing around one favorite word as if it were going out of style: "no." "No," they whined, when I told them to drink their milk at dinner. "No," they shouted, when it was naptime. "No," they protested, crying great big crocodile tears when I said it was time to turn off the television.

But then there were the no's for all the times when I tried to help them climb the stairs or put their shoes on, when they wanted to do these things for themselves. These no's, even if they expressed a desire for independence from the Great Chief Mother of the

---

2. I'm grateful to friend Lindsey Horton for sharing these recollections on Facebook and letting me use them here.

3. Lewis, *The Problem of Pain*, 88–89.

Frazzled Hair, were not the militant, war cries of rebels. These no's were healthy forms of self-expression from little people who needed to grow, learn, and adapt to their environment.

Even as a grownup, I know how this is. Every once in a while my husband will try to do something for me when I am trying to do it for myself and have grown frustrated. That is when I need to say "back off." For all the times I may happily permit my husband to open car doors for me, move large, heavy objects, or, like my personal sherpa, carry the bulkier, more burdensome backpack on hiking trips, there are also the occasions when I'm trying to read an instruction manual or cook something more complex than a frozen dinner from Trader Joe's. In those times, when I want to do the thing for myself, nothing can be more unhelpful than to be relieved of a challenge I alone wish to tackle.

In other words, sometimes our no's can be very healthy expressions of our need for space—a space in which to discover who we are, what we want and how God made us. A space for learning what we can and cannot do. A space in which to negotiate our limits and aptitudes. A space in which to become ourselves.

The truth is that we all need at least a few car lengths between our vehicle and another to make it to our end destination in one piece.

Sometimes, we really do just need to say "no" for both our own good and for our neighbor's; but for many of us, this healthy manifestation of "no" tends to fade as we grow older, with many of us finding it more and more difficult to voice our need for boundaries. The boss who exploits your time and treats you like a punching bag every time he loses his temper. The next-door neighbor whose dog is perpetually taking a dump on your yard. The friend who really needs a therapist but instead calls you daily to unload her problems. Such boundary violations can be hard to resist.

This reality gained confirmation not long ago, when I and another mother were asked to guard the entrance to the auditorium before the start of the annual holiday performance put on by my son's school. "Winterfest," as it is called, is one of those nights when moms and dads have an excuse to dress up their little Billy or Susie in a tie or poofy, red dress and take pictures of their children singing sweet, anodyne songs about the season's festivities. And the kids always look adorable—maybe most especially because in every performance there are always a few on stage who, as they play their recorders, ring bells, or lip sync to "Jingle Bells," look like they would rather be visiting the dentist or organizing their sock drawer.

That night I had been asked to don a loud, orange shirt that distinguished me as one of the official parent volunteers, and my task seemed clear enough: to keep several hundred eager parents from following their children into the main auditorium and grabbing seats before the doors to the performance had been officially opened. My new partner and I were to put on our best smiles and politely invite arriving parents to visit the refreshments stand or wait leisurely in the lobby until we gave the cue to enter. Our job, I had assumed, would be a bit like that of those kind-sounding senior citizens at the opera who gently direct newcomers to their seat.

Only a few brief encounters disabused me of this preconception, however. To stand for a whole half hour between parents and their claim on a good seat from which to photograph their children, I quickly discovered, requires more of the skill set of a trained bouncer or police officer. There was the uncle from out of town who whined that five previous knee surgeries required a seat inside the auditorium and looked especially put out when I invited him to sit in the lobby. Or the fashionably dressed, skinny redhead who, clutching her kids to her side, barged her way in with not so much as even a polite acknowledgment that she was somehow an exception to the rule.

Then there were all of the other parents who innocently said they only wanted to escort their children to their seat; after that, went the claim, they would come right back out and join the rest of the law-abiding newcomers standing patiently at the entrance. This excuse proved quite effective, even if it seemed a bit dubious from the start; there was something fishy about the fact that these parents could not entrust their sweet Billy or Susie to another parent usher who would walk the child the full length of twenty-five yards to the stage where their class sat waiting. At one point in the proceedings, my fellow bouncer and I turned to survey the success of our efforts: a growing cluster of newcomers had found comfortable seats inside the auditorium, while the rest of the pack still standing at the entrance beheld the grave injustice taking place before their eyes.

In no time I was giving thanks I had not pursued a career in law enforcement.

Jesus knew how to assert clear boundaries. In the face of an unrelenting workload and all manner of demands on his time, he would often find a private place to which to retire in prayer and solitude. Forty days in the wilderness alone launched Jesus's ministry; it took separating himself from life's many and various, competing distractions to set out on the path of being the person God called him to be.

Learning to carve out our own space is, I suspect, one critical aspect to following in Jesus's path. This process also helps us better hear our soul speak. The older I get, the more I'm convinced these two things are related—that following Jesus means tending to our souls, by learning to listen and respond to those inner grumblings, stirrings and hunger pangs. This intentionality is both hard and necessary if we wish to become who God wants us to be.

"Men try to dissuade me from everything Love bids me do," wrote the thirteenth-century Beguine, poet, and theologian Hadewijch of Antwerp. "They don't understand it, and I can't explain it to them. I must live out what I am."[4] And, Hadewijch of all people would know what it means to claim a room of one's own in which to hear the soul speak: she was one of a roaming community of women who, in devoting themselves to prayer, chastity and service, eschewed the more traditional routes laid out to them in their time, even enduring imprisonment, persecution, and martyrdom as a result. Finding the freedom to "live out what we are" cannot happen apart from an articulation of our own space and boundaries.

---

4. "Beguines" were itinerant, self-sufficient, self-governing communities of women devoted to the spiritual life; unlike nuns, they did not submit to orders and were not bound by vows. "They existed somewhere between the world and the cloister, in a state of autonomy which was highly unusual for medieval women and highly disturbing to medieval men," according to an obituary in 2012 of Marcella Putyn, the last of the Beguines. See The Economist Group, "Marcella Putyn," 86. The quote from Hadewijch is found in Hadewijch, *Hadewijch*, 186.

BOUNDARIES AS THE BEGINNING OF COMMUNITY

Something else happens, though, in carving out my own space. The act of expressing my boundaries presumes there is also a space between myself and another human being. This respect for the distance between you and me is, I suspect, the beginning of true intimacy, and true intimacy fosters real community.

Finding community like this is priceless, both because this kind of safe transparency between human beings really is so rare, and because such honesty is as risky as it is transformative. When I'm feeling confused about a direction to take or overwhelmed by circumstances, that is when I turn to a few dear friends who know me through and through. They form an informal, miniature support group, a small circle of trusted friends in which our mutual confession to one another becomes the stuff of prayer for and with one another—so that together we might connect with our own inner wholeness.[5]

In his book *The Hidden Wholeness*, Parker Palmer posits that "a still, small voice" is always telling us who we are and what direction to take, despite our ingenious capacity to ignore that voice.[6]

"I hear [the voice] and yet act as if I did not," Palmer writes. "I withhold a personal gift that might serve a good end or commit myself to a project that I do not really believe in. I keep silent on an issue I should address or actively break faith with one of my own convictions. I deny an inner darkness, giving it more power over me, or I project it onto other people, creating 'enemies' where none exist."[7]

For Parker, learning to listen to this still, small voice begins with the cultivating of solitude and mutual attentiveness within intentional community. Parker calls this mode of relating to one another and to our own selves a "circle of trust."[8] Participants in a circle of trust must agree to be more willing to listen than to speak,

---

5. James 5:16: "Confess your sins to one another and pray for one another so that you might be healed."
6. Palmer, *The Hidden Wholeness*, 4.
7. Ibid.
8. Ibid., 52–57.

more quick to withhold judgment than to condemn, more eager to learn than to teach, and more willing to be changed than bent on changing others.[9] And, in order to listen to the inner teacher that is our soul, we need a safe space in which to hear one another, one that is founded on a carefully applied principle of non-judgmental respect for ourselves and for one another.

These sacred or holy spaces are a fundamental requirement for any circle of trust to survive or thrive. Spaces set apart from the dog-eat-dog routines of the world in which we live are the very sites where a crucified God lets us survey both our shared brokenness and God's work in and through us. The holiest spaces are those where we have come to see the interconnectedness of our sin and sickness and our part in one another's redemption; where a quickness to judge has given way to pure, mutual acceptance, because God has first accepted us. Authentic community requires holy space: these two things go together.

Adam Copeland is a Presbyterian pastor in young adult ministry in the Fargo-Moorhead area of North Dakota and Minnesota. He recently voiced the challenge he faces in his work of reaching the next generation: in his area alone, there are scores of churches, but 45,000 young adults, representing nearly a quarter of the entire population there, are not connected to any of these churches.[10]

This conundrum obliged Copeland to do something many of us ministers are not so good at: "I listen a lot and talk very little," Copeland shared in an article in *The Christian Century*.[11] Copeland listened to the stories of these young people, and as he listened, he perceived something between the lines of what they were saying. "What I was hearing, over and over again," Copeland wrote, "was . . . a longing for a space in which nascent faith could be nurtured without judgment."[12]

---

9. Ibid.
10. Adam Copeland, "No need for church," para. 1.
11. Ibid., para. 3.
12. Ibid., para. 7.

There was the gal who had grown up in the church but felt pushed out when she revealed her sexuality.[13]

There was the guy who had once considered becoming a youth pastor in the church only to find the rigidity of his conservative evangelical denomination unwelcoming to his questions about the Bible and theology.[14]

There was the young woman who simply wanted a safe space in which to voice her questions and grow in loving God and neighbor.[15]

In each of these lives, holy space had been lacking—a well-protected, safe space set apart for simply being oneself and exploring and asking one's questions, without the judgment of pat answers or lofty prescriptions for so-called right belief from theological experts.

In listening to these stories, Copeland was transformed, his whole approach to ministry being the most evident sign of that transformation. Now Copeland sees a big part of his role in reaching young adults as one of simply providing safe settings in which to ask questions, listen to one another, form friendships, and relax in conversation. You might characterize his approach as cultivating holy spaces.

It seems to me that Copeland and Palmer are on to something. I suspect that what the world needs today is less tailgating in the form of bold prescriptions for theologically correct belief or right living.

What the world needs is a church willing to listen. To be attentive to the world around her. To wait and watch and testify to how God leads.

What the world needs are more holy spaces and circles of trust, and people willing to cultivate them.

In that process, maybe more of us will discover that God is already at work. Maybe more of us will come to see that we don't have to bring God to the world, because God has already been there

---

13. Ibid., para. 4.
14. Ibid., para. 5.
15. Ibid., para. 6.

all along. Thankfully, God was there well before we got there, and God will be there long after we leave.

DISCUSSION QUESTIONS

1. Would you ever put the bumper sticker, "If you can read this, you are too close," on your car? Why or why not? How have you usually interpreted this bumper sticker?

2. How are boundaries and space related? Is there a tension between boundaries and space? How might issues of boundaries and space positively and negatively impact the life of individuals and/or the church?

3. Are you familiar with the Ten Commandments? How were you first introduced to them? What preconceptions, if any, have you harbored about the character of a God who issues commandments?

4. Do you agree that the Ten Commandments are there for our own good and flourishing? Why or why not? Which commandments do you find hardest to follow? Which commandments have you found easiest to follow?

5. When was the last time you really listened to your own soul speak? What did you discover?

6. Can you recall a time from your own life in which you found yourself in a holy space similar to the kind that Copeland and Palmer are being intentional about creating? How did the experience impact you?

7. What are the risks and possibilities posed for the church, do you think, in creating holy spaces? What are ways that your church might create holy spaces? How would you need to rethink church in order to create such holy spaces?

4

DON'T LET MY CAR FOOL YOU MY TREASURE IS IN HEAVEN

> *Our destination is an earthly one: a new earth, an earth redeemed and transfigured. An earth reunited with heaven, but an earth, nevertheless.*
>
> —Paul Marshall

> *Behold the dwelling of God is with them. He will dwell with them, and they shall be his people and God himself will be with them; He will wipe away every tear from their eyes, and death shall be no more, neither shall there be mourning nor crying nor pain anymore, for the former things have passed away.*
>
> —Revelation 21:3, 4

The Way

Usually when I see this bumper sticker, it is on the back of the luxury SUV or sports car with all the accessories, but when Facebook friends weighed in with their favorite bumper stickers, one friend volunteered that she had seen these same words over the tailpipes of cars that could only be described as treasure for the local junkyard. The ratty Pinto with the peeling paint job, maybe. Or the bound-for-retirement banana boat.

Or, just maybe, that endearingly strappy, red hatchback Datsun that saw our family through my father's graduate school days upon our return from the mission field in Malaysia. Those were some of the happiest, most magical days of my childhood—no matter that we lived in cockroach-infested student housing in an apartment stocked with furniture from the Salvation Army, or that I had to share not just a small room but a bunk bed with my younger brother; no matter that we regularly subsisted on egg soufflés and processed macaroni and cheese, my mother stretching every penny of our weekly grocery budget of fifty dollars to feed a family of five.

In those days, before the onset of puberty would steal a child's carefree unselfconsciousness, I would ride my rusty, ten-speed bicycle all around the neighborhood, dropping in on playmates or stopping to swing on the monkey bars at the local playground. Or I would head for the weeping willow tree just down the street, to climb in its branches and simply daydream. That bicycle became a trusty friend.

But nothing could rival the steady reliability of that good old hatchback Datsun with the tired, black vinyl interior and the get-up of a little engine that thought it could (and did). That car had also survived the two-week trip across the country that had landed us there, in New Haven, Connecticut, all the way from Los Angeles. It was a trip punctuated by daily stops at McDonalds, a younger brother's frequent complaints of being tormented by yours truly, and then, somewhere before crossing the Mason-Dixon line, the announcement that my mother was expecting my youngest brother.

"Children," my dad had announced smilingly, his eyes rather gleefully landing on us through the rear-view mirror as he gave my mother's leg one of his meaningful squeezes, "your mom is going to have a baby."

Don't Let My Car Fool You. My Treasure Is in Heaven

And when I, now a mother myself, recall that trip, I can only marvel at the patience that such an odyssey must have required of this long-suffering woman whose maternal role I once rather dismissively regarded. Driving cross-country in that cramped, little hatch back, while still in the throes of first-trimester morning sickness, with two annoying, obstreperous, pre-adolescent children in the back seat, would have been enough to elicit a request to be dropped off at the local spa. Like in those Calgon commercials from the 1980s: the frazzled housewife, upon opening the door to her children's room and to a cloud of feathers and the mayhem of a pillow fight, sighs wistfully and, staring longingly into the camera, exclaims, "Calgon, take me away!—only to be quickly transported to a luxurious, bubble bath surrounded by ethereal light.

Heaven in a beauty bar.

Or . . . the nearest escape route from Planet Earth.

Like the very last lifeboat waiting to be untethered from a sinking Titanic.

I used to think that when Jesus says he is the Way, and that he is taking those willing to follow to a mansion with many rooms, he is talking about this sort of heaven. Heaven for lifeboat evacuees and desperate housewives. Heaven as another place entirely from an earth hurtling towards some final, permanent cosmic wipe-out. Heaven as a last-ditch rescue plan in the face of an apocalyptic, global warming that burns up all the damned left to tough it out on Planet Earth in one terrible, eternal conflagration.

This nearest emergency exit for the so-called saved was the same pearly-gated place I once had heard about growing up in Sunday School classes and at summer church camps. This version of heaven was only a bit less caricature-like than its spoof by the humor magazine *The Onion* some years back: as they ascend to the clouds in an escalator, caught up in the Rapture, all of the right-wing fundamentalists, including a prominently displayed Pat Robertson, wave smiling "goodbyes" to the damned below with the sign-off, "So long, suckers"; only in my case, the metaphorical "escalator" usually looked more like the Sinner's Prayer, repeated after some charismatic youth pastor's invitation, as if to seal the deal.[1]

This heaven was where our *real* treasure would be. Everything in the earthly journey was at best, preparation for, and at worst, in diabolical conflict with, this end destination.

"Where your treasure is, there your heart is also," Jesus says.[2]

Our hearts were to be set on this heavenly finishing line, because that is where our real treasure was.

BEYOND RABBIT HOLES

There was once a time when I felt guilty for intuitively appreciating how the earth and the journey itself so beautifully got in the way.

Not anymore.

The finest things in this life, things like truth and beauty, love and joy, mystery and wonder, are, I believe, expressions of heaven on earth. A God who in Jesus Christ has wed himself with all creation and cannot let it go makes these things reason enough to keep our feet firmly grounded on this earth, taking good care of it, tilling its soil, and celebrating our creatureliness.

We were meant to enjoy the scenery along life's road, taking in the views, stopping for ice cream, and playing silly license plate games along the way. In the same way we were made for an earthly paradise, we are also meant to delight in creation here and now. We were intended "to enjoy God forever," and we do this by falling in love with the beautiful, fragile world God knitted together at the beginning of time and called "good."[3]

I suspect we were also built with an internal Global Positioning System of sorts that causes us to seek out the Way—to ask and wonder where we are ultimately going as we take in the sights of the Grand Canyon or a beautiful coastline.

---

1. Dikkers, ed., "Christian Right Ascends to Heaven," *Our Dumb Century*, 164.

2. Matthew 6:21.

3. In the words of "The Shorter Westminster Catechism," "man's chief aim is to glorify God and enjoy Him forever." See the Presbyterian Church, *The Constitution of the Presbyterian Church (U.S.A.)*, Part 1, 175.

What is our purpose?
What are we here for?
What is our end destination?

Can we really enjoy the scenery if we are convinced that the Way requires we never stop to appreciate the colors of a rainbow or the texture of a flower petal? Or that all creation is attached to some ticking time bomb that will one day detonate? Or that the only answer to these existential questions is the last-minute lifeboat or the "Aha!" escalator?

Maybe Jesus knew we human beings have a tendency to look for easy rabbit holes and quick-fix solutions. Maybe for this same reason, when he teaches his disciples to pray, he tells them to pray, "Thy kingdom come . . . on earth as it is in heaven." He tells them to ask for God's perfectly good will to reign in the here and now. On Planet Earth, not somewhere else altogether.

In other words, Jesus is telling his disciples to keep their sights not on some magical, pie-in-the-sky, other-worldly realm. Jesus is urging them to pray and wholeheartedly seek now for the reunification of heaven and earth, when every dimension of creation and the cosmos is finally in alignment with the will of its Creator, when God reigns over all things and in all things.[4]

Rob Bell sums it up this way in his bestselling book, *Love Wins:*

> What Jesus taught,
> what the prophets taught,
> what all of Jewish tradition pointed to
> and what Jesus lived in anticipation of,
> was the day when earth and heaven would be one.
> The day when God's will would be done on earth
> as it is now done in heaven.
> The day when earth and heaven *will be the same place.*[5]

---

4. Colossians 1:17–19.
5. Bell, *Love Wins*, 42–43.

The Way

TREASURE ON EARTH AS IT IS IN HEAVEN

"Go, sell what you own, and give the money to the poor," Jesus tells the rich man who asks Jesus what he must do to inherit eternal life. "Then you will have treasure in heaven."[6]

"Treasure in heaven" not just some day, but now. The more you're able to live freely today, your hands open and ready to receive God's gifts rather than clutching fearfully to your possessions, the better positioned you will be to enter into unending life tomorrow. The more generous with your earthly treasures you can be now, letting go of those things that would seek to imprison you rather than set you free to follow where God leads, the closer you will already be to "that day when earth and heaven will be the same place." The more deeply you will experience that coming reality not just in the life to come but *now*. This very moment.

If, as Bell writes, "heaven is that place where things are as God intends them to be," "eternal life" is our participation in those things.[7] And if I'm honest with myself, that reality is what I most want. Not just some day but here and now. In the stuff of real life. Right now.

At times I have caught glimpses, albeit fleeting ones, of this heavenly treasure.

Serving a meal at a shelter for homeless women.

Worshiping across traditions with people who look very different from me.

Finding forgiveness and reconciliation in a broken relationship.

Experiencing the magic of discovery all over again through the eyes of my children, and watching as their faces light up with wonder and joy.

Laughter.

Peace.

Freedom.

The rich man walks away sadly, because he loves his wealth too much, and cannot let it go; and here is the catch: you and I

---

6. Matthew 19:16–30; Mark 10:17–31; Luke 18:18–30.
7. Bell, *Love Wins*, 42.

cannot, either. Only a God for whom "all things are possible" can take us there, and Jesus says, "I am the Way."[8]

"Follow me."

The tragedy of the rich young man is that he sees the Way right in front of him and rejects It. The "More" that he lacks is imminently available, and he chooses to turn his back on It. Jesus gives him this choice, and the man picks the safety and security of material riches over the far more exhilarating, more life-giving alternative.

In the end there may not be that much difference between this man and another who stars notoriously in one of Jesus's many parables. This second character builds a big barn to store all his earthly treasure, only to discover that when he dies he will lose everything in one fell stroke. The story itself is fictional; but its lesson—that wealth is fickle and its accumulation in this life simply for the sake of it, foolish—plays out all over the place.

A more contemporary case in point? David and Jackie Siegel, whose real-life story inspired the recent documentary, *Queen of Versailles*. Before the 2008 stock market crash, they were ambitiously constructing what was to be the largest home in modern America. The 90,000 foot house would hold thirty bathrooms, ten kitchens, a bowling alley, a sushi bar, two tennis courts and a full-size baseball field, for starters, and would be filled to the brim with Louis XIV-style furniture—hence, the nomenclature of a modern-day "Versailles." Almost overnight, though, the Siegels saw their American Dream on steroids spontaneously combust as stocks hit rock-bottom and the housing market crashed.

The Siegels' dizzying reversal of fortune is more than just a cautionary morality tale about the dangers of American excess and consumption. There is an implicit reality at play here that brings into question the trustworthiness of store barns and wannabe Versailles palaces, calling them out as dead ends: "real treasure in heaven." The "Kingdom of God" is another name for it.

Where heaven and earth kiss each other, where God dwells among us and we in God, and where God wipes away every tear:

---

8. Matthew 19:26.

this kingdom of God is a dynamic reality.[9] At any moment, you and I can choose to believe this kingdom of God is right in front of us and to step into it; or, we, like the rich man, can turn our backs and walk away.

The invitation here is to invest in that which "moths and rust cannot destroy and thieves do not break in and steal."[10] Our earthly treasures only really have lasting value to the degree that they are caught up in God's great, big work of bringing heaven and earth back together in a long-awaited reunion. The question is, do we *want* to be part of that consummation? Do we want to step into God's reconciliation of all things and join in the meaningful action that brings us life that won't run out?

Do we really want to inherit eternal life?

The Way is open before us. The Way who has no place to lay his head and who bids us come along, this same one says, "See, I am making all things new," and, "I am going ahead of you to prepare a place for you."[11]

That makes me want to follow.

DISCUSSION QUESTIONS

1. *Do Kristina's earliest introductions to heaven—as a convenient escape route or eternal vacation spot for the saved—resonate? Why or why not? How, if at all, were you first introduced to heaven? Has that understanding changed, and if so, how?*

2. *Where in your world do you most see evidence of heaven on earth? How does it make you want to be part of it?*

3. *Read the story of the rich young man in its three versions (Matthew, Luke, and Mark). What do you make of Jesus's expression, "treasure in heaven," here? What is the rich young man missing out on? Why do you think he walks away?*

---

9. Bell, *Love Wins*, 43–44.
10. Matthew 6:20.
11. Revelation 21:5; John 14:3.

4. How, if at all, does Kristina's description of the "kingdom of God" and "heavenly treasure" cause you to rethink your understanding of heaven and earth?

5. What is your earthly treasure, and why? What about it might be an expression of "heaven on earth"? How might your earthly treasure take part in that Divine Project to reunify heaven and earth that Kristina describes?

5

HONK IF YOU LOVE JESUS
TEXT IF YOU WANT TO MEET HIM

[Worship] is not for the timid or comfortable. It involves an opening of our selves to the adventurous life of the Spirit.
—RICHARD FOSTER

With what shall I come before the Lord, and bow myself before God on high? Shall I come before him with burnt offerings, with calves a year old? Will the Lord be pleased with thousands of rams, with ten thousands of rivers of oil? Shall I give my firstborn for my transgression, the fruit of my body for the sin of my soul?" He has told you, O mortal, what is good; and what does the Lord require of you but to do justice, and to love kindness, and to walk humbly with your God?

—MICAH 6:6–8

Honk if You Love Jesus. Text if You Want to Meet Him

TEXTING WHILE DRIVING IS now against the law in most states, which makes meeting Jesus illegal by the standards of this bumper sticker; and the last time I honked at someone was not because I wanted to express my love for Jesus.

But what if the sentiments here were also a reminder—a reminder that worship is not just something we do in our sacred spaces?

Because if we think worship is only the ceremonial, religious dress-up many of us play on any given Sunday morning in churches across America, or pretty sounding words from a preacher, or our favorite hymns, we will be surprised, or disappointed, or ecstatic, when God overturns our preconceptions.

Maybe we'll be surprised, disappointed, and ecstatic all at the same time.

Because if God can't be kept in church, neither can our worship. If God can't be reduced to the once-weekly fill-up station for our spiritual tanks, neither can our exclamation when we find God out on life's open road with us.

And if you've ever gazed at the sky on a clear, dark night, marveling at the billions of stars in the Milky Way galaxy and the billions more in the billions of galaxies beyond ours, then you'll know what I'm talking about: chances are your jaw dropped, agape in awe and wonder at the magnitude of our universe and your own smallness in it.[1] If you've ever stopped to marvel at your own unique fingerprints or the birth of a child, or been awoken by pain or heartbreak to a desire for answers beyond yourself and a meaning that holds together this fragile universe, you can identify. You can understand what I mean when I ponder whether worship, as a capacity to respond with awe, wonder and child-like exclamation—or, even lament—to the unexplainable Otherness that has knit us and our world together, is not fundamental to human existence.

"We are such stuff as dreams are made on, and our little life is rounded with a sleep," Prospero declares in Shakespeare's play *The*

---

1. These reflections have been reprinted with the permission of *Beliefnet*. See Kristina Robb-Dover, "The Wise Men 'Tebowed,'" Fellowship of Saints and Sinners, *Beliefnet*, para. 4.

Tempest.[2] Maybe worship in its most basic sense is a similar exclamation—the kind that reminds us of the possibility and limitation, the glory and humiliation of being human in the first place.

Worship in this sense is not a religious or Christian act: it is part and parcel of being human. If we're not honking our love for Jesus or texting if we want to meet him, we are, by virtue of being human, "bowing down" to something or someone.

The question the Bible poses is not whether we will worship, but *what* we will worship. From what do we derive our identity, purpose and sense of direction? What is our *Way*?

Money?

Power?

Achievement?

A relationship?

Our own selves?

These are the Bible's "golden calves," before these came to mean the shapely, sun-kissed leg muscles you flex at the gym.

Like the big golden bull the Israelites erect in the wilderness, these false gods are our own well-meaning attempts to find a substitute for God; and, anything that lets us tell ourselves lies about who we are, or who God is, qualifies.[3]

In nearly forty years of life, I've discovered my own relentless capacity to idolize just about anything.

A relationship.

Comfort.

Health.

Pedigree.

Control.

Bruce Springsteen.

We could go on, but then the length of my list might rival Martin Luther's *95 Theses*.

If such false gods seem like safer, easier, or more exciting paths to take in the short-term, they ultimately take us nowhere. They are like a great big cry for directions.

---

2. Shakespeare, *The Tempest*, *The Complete Works of William Shakespeare*, IV.1, 17.

3. Exodus 32.

WORSHIP AS TRANSFORMATIONAL ENCOUNTER

There must have been something so irresistible about Jesus that made the first disciples follow his directions, after their very first encounter with this stranger.

The Gospel of Luke records how after a long, unsuccessful night trying to catch fish, Peter and his exhausted crew reluctantly put out their nets one last time—this time because Jesus tells them to. And this time their nets emerge bursting at the seams with fish, so much so that Peter's gut reaction is to "fall down on his knees" and exclaim, "'Go away from me, Lord, for I am a sinful man!'"[4]

"Worship," as Mark Labberton puts it, in his book *The Dangerous Act of Worship*, is what happens in an "encounter" with "the true and living God."[5] And if we're unsure about whether we're encountering God himself, one clue to look for, according to Luke, will be if we find ourselves on our knees asking God to leave, but then following God anyway.

You might call it "holy schizophrenia."

John Ortberg has called it "the knee-buckling, jaw-dropping acknowledgment of the gap between the creature and the Creator, the finite and the Infinite, the sinful and the Holy."[6]

Peter and his mates in an instant recognize both God and their need for Him, and within moments of this instant recognition, they "immediately" leave not just their boats but "everything" to follow Jesus, because from now on, Jesus has given them a new vocation— "catching people," Jesus calls it.

The whole enterprise is crazy, really. I mean, since when did you ask the question, "What do you do?" to get the answer, "I catch people?"

"I sell insurance." Okay.

"I teach swim lessons." Yes.

But "I catch people"? Usually when I hear anything remotely similar to that expression, I think "human trafficking." Or law enforcement to the tune of the long-running television series, *Cops*,

---

4. Luke 5:8
5. Labberton, *The Dangerous Act of Worship*, 63.
6. Foreword to ibid., 9.

a family favorite growing up: there was a time when every Friday night for some unexplainable reason we used to gather around the tube with a big bowl of popcorn to watch real-life police officers apprehend pimps, prostitutes, and drug dealers in undercover busts, or track criminals in dramatic, high-speed car chases.

But catching people with the disarming love of God and introducing them to Someone worthy of their worship and a purpose for their lives? Not so much. Most people I know don't *choose* this sort of job description.

The disciples follow Jesus, anyway. They're as caught as the fish they've been pulling up in nets all these years. Something in Jesus is so compelling that they cannot do anything but follow. Even if it means a sudden change in job description. Even if from now on they'll never be able to answer the question, "What do you do?" without eliciting raised eyebrows, curious looks, or discomfited shuffling.

If worship on life's open road happens spontaneously, without our having to manufacture it, such worship is also risky, to the degree that it hooks and catches us, overturning our priorities, transforming our aspirations, and asking for nothing less than our everything. Anywhere, at any moment, the one, true, living God can issue directions, so that we're never the same again—so that we choose to trade in our way for God's way, putting one foot in front of the other right behind Jesus. Sure, we'll stumble. Sure, we may have to stop to catch our breath. We may even turn around and exclaim in despair, "I give up." But ultimately we will not be able to return to *just* catching fish or selling insurance or teaching swim lessons. We won't be able to because somewhere along life's way we met God, fell on our knees and asked God to leave. And God didn't obey. And that is when we'll know that the only thing we really can do is follow.

That is how it happened for my granddad at least.

"Granddad John," as he is endearingly known by his family, was a big-shot corporate lawyer with a well-established reputation in the prime of his life, when one night Jesus came to him and told him to follow.

My granddad had been teaching Sunday school for many years, but as he recalls, he hadn't really encountered Jesus until that night. He hadn't really grappled with the implications for his life of a God "over all and through all and in all" until this reality had become uncomfortably personal.[7]

That night, under the dark expanse of a New Mexico sky and in the solitariness of his Buick station wagon, alone with his thoughts and this God, my granddad spent hours driving rural back roads on the outskirts of his hometown Albuquerque, wrestling with the implications of the encounter. By morning he had relinquished himself to the fact that his life would never be the same again.

And it never was.

In the years to come, my granddad would devote himself to the work of providing legal aid to homeless and under-served persons in this country, so that even now, in his late eighties, Granddad John spends his most joy-filled hours providing free legal advice to the poor and advocating tirelessly on behalf of this nation's most vulnerable, legally disenfranchised populations.

"Worship," as Labberton puts it, is the "dangerous act of waking up to God and God's purposes in this world and living out God's call to justice."[8] If Jesus is the Way, worship is both an encounter with this Way and our following of directions. By this definition, worship is much more risky than texting while driving, sounds much more beautiful than honking your love for Jesus, only sometimes actually happens in church, and . . . will paint our world in the colors of heaven.

The last book of the Bible, Revelation, envisions the heavenliness of a world illuminated by a 24/7 encounter with the living God:

> a great multitude that no one [can] count, from every nation, from all tribes and peoples and languages . . . are before the throne of God, and worship him day and night within his temple, and the one who is seated on the throne [Jesus] will shelter them. They will hunger no more, and thirst no more; the sun will not strike them, nor any scorching heat; for the Lamb at the center of the

---

7. Ephesians 4:6.
8. Labberton, *The Dangerous Act of Worship*, 13.

throne will be their shepherd, and he will guide them to springs of the water of life, and God will wipe away every tear from their eyes.[9]

No more pain. No more tears. No more hunger or drought or famine. Only God on God's throne, at the center of all things, surrounded by throngs of worshiping people. Their songs fill the temple that is God's world day and night—all because they have met Jesus and have come to know and love him.

DISCUSSION QUESTIONS

1. *What first impressions come to mind when you see this bumper sticker? Is it meant to be tongue in cheek?*
2. *What was your most "worship-full" moment and why?*
3. *What keeps you from encountering God in worship and why?*
4. *How is worship risky? What are you most afraid of?*
5. *Kristina lists a number of so-called golden calves—false gods that can sometimes signify our preferred mode of direction. What are your false gods? How do they keep you from taking the Way, insofar as that Way calls you to a life of service to God and your world?*
6. *When was the last time God overturned your preconceptions that worship only happens in church?*
7. *How might you encounter God more on life's open road if you are not already?*

---

9. Revelation 7:9–17.

6

God Is My CO-PILOT

God was my co-pilot, but we crashed in the mountains and I had to eat him.

—The bumper sticker on a pick-up truck at a traffic light in front of me.

There are two kinds of people: those who say to God, "Thy will be done," and those to whom God says, "All right, then, have it your way."

—C. S. Lewis

In my early twenties, I flew to Moscow, Russia with a view to exploring a future in freelance reporting for the ABC News bureau there. The flight was especially memorable. The pilot was a

The Way

Frenchman with a knack for showing off his aviation skills to young women.

As the plane was preparing for a descent into Paris for a stopover, one of the pilot's flight attendants summoned me with the following invitation in an endearing French accent: "Ze pilot would like to know if you would like to fly in ze cockpit while we land."

I didn't hesitate. "Sure!" I readily volunteered.

What ensued was rather surreal. I found myself in the co-pilot seat, headphones on, surveying the rolling French countryside while listening to the pilot spend far too much time talking to his young female companion rather than preparing for landing.

The dialogue, made that much more comedic by the pilot's broken English and my broken French, went something as follows:

Air France Pilot: "Do you like James Bond?"

Me: "Yes." (I had to be honest: to this day I still nurse the dream of one day becoming a Bond girl.)

Air France Pilot: "Well, I can be your James Bond if you would like."

At this juncture, my pilot—the guy I had assumed was to be landing our plane in literally just a few minutes—proceeded to pull out a photo album and show me pictures of himself taken all around the world.

There was my pilot next to his yacht.

There he was again scuba diving at a coral reef.

There he was on the Swiss ski slopes.

I was impressed—and more by the fact that my pilot was expecting me to be more interested in his photo album (a.k.a. playbook) than whether our plane would safely land.

Thankfully, our plane did safely touch the tarmac at Charles de Gaulle airport; but if our landing was successful, that pilot's invitation to spend the night in Paris with him was less so. I politely turned it down. Still, I was glad to have served as co-pilot—so long as I wasn't expected to land the plane.

WANNABE SOLO PILOTS

It is easy to deceive ourselves that we are in the cockpit with God. Sure, we may pay lip service to the idea that God governs our lives. If we believe in Jesus, we may even call him "Lord." But when push comes to shove, we would prefer to sit up front, pretending we are really at the controls.

This dynamic can play out in how we approach scripture as the Word of God. I suspect most of us are prone to read the Bible as we would prefer to read it. You don't have to pull a Thomas Jefferson and cut out all of the parts of the Bible you find unsavory in order to appreciate the ways in which we in all manner of ways can conscript scripture for our own agendas. For all the times when scripture is confusing, contradictory, and difficult to interpret—and there are many—there are those occasions when the meaning is as plain as day and we would prefer that it not be. So we pull intellectual Houdini acts: we writhe, bend, and pry ourselves free from any radical, convicting claim of God on our lives that might require too much inconvenience or sacrifice on our parts. One example? "Love your neighbor as yourself." Some of the plainest put advice in the Bible can be the hardest to put into action and therefore the easiest to ignore, deconstruct, or explain away.

I suppose our hard-wired propensity to grab the controls stems from an amazing knack for self-deception. Our hearts find it easy to indulge illusions as if they were reality itself. The Book of Jeremiah warns that the human heart is "deceitful above all things and desperately wicked."[1]

When we deceive ourselves into thinking that we were made to fly the plane, we reduce God's presence and power to that of a pretty passenger who never went to aviation school. We invite God along for the ride, sure, but in reality we would never hand God the controls. We go about life as if God's function is nothing more than to keep us company as we pilot our private jet.

Which is a life-threatening problem when we really do not know how to fly the plane in the first place.

---

1. Jeremiah 7:9.

The Way

Scripture is chock-full of people who thought they could fly solo only to discover they were wrong. One of my favorites is Jonah. His story would make that television documentary series *I Shouldn't Be Alive* seem tame: the mind-boggling, death-defying survival stories of people who have been bitten by black mambas in the African bush or have spent days and weeks shipwrecked in shark-ridden waters could not hold a candle to the suspense of spending three days and three nights in the belly of a whale.

Jonah, like many of us, is a wannabe solo pilot. When God tells him to go to the city of Ninevah and "cry out against it" because of its "wickedness," Jonah literally runs in the other direction, boarding a ship to "flee from the presence of the Lord."[2] The guy who thought he could do life on his own ends up being thrown overboard and becoming the next meal of some great big fish. Only when he finds himself sitting waist high in a whale's stomach bile, maybe wedged somewhere between a dorsal fin and a tail with a nasty case of seasickness to boot, does Jonah hand over the whole operation to God.

Whenever we find that we have grabbed the controls only to crash and burn or wipe out, it may be helpful to remember Jonah, because things could always be worse. We could be whale bait.

LETTING GO OF THE CONTROLS

The truth of the matter is that we human beings all need a Pilot. Not one of us has a license to fly. We might convince ourselves that we do. We might like how we look at the controls, or enjoy the rush of being in charge or having it all together, or relish the sound of air traffic control in our headphones, but not one of us can ultimately guide the plane. From lift-off to landing we are in the hands of the One who made us and holds us in his hands, like in that old poem, "Footprints in the Sand," which I used to see everywhere growing up. The poem usually came affixed to a photo of some sunset-swept beach and was available for purchase in just about any Christian bookstore. The poet wonders, as she walks along the beach with

---

2. Jonah 1:2–3.

God, as to why in times of great trial or duress she notices only one set of footprints in the sand, whereas elsewhere she sees two pairs. The answer comes back: in the hard times God has carried her. Kind of treacly and insipid, but true nonetheless.

A beautiful thing happens when we let go of the controls and let God be in charge—when we begin to confess over and over again that God carries us and that God alone is the Pilot. The more we submit ourselves to God, asking God to shape us into the people God would have us be, the closer we find ourselves to the Pilot and the clearer our view of the world becomes.[3] The more we're able to make out the contours of the landscape before us and take in its beauty and blemishes. The better we're able to hear the Pilot's directions and warnings, as well as the Pilot's praises. "Well done, good and faithful servant," we may even hear the Pilot say.

In his memoir *All Is Grace*, author and former Catholic priest Brennan Manning describes the life-changing experience of befriending one person who had completely surrendered his life to God. In the late 1960s, Manning had taken a leave of absence from the Franciscans to live and work alongside the Little Brothers of Jesus, in Saint-Rémy, France. The Brothers are not a cloistered monastic order: they are committed to a daily life of prayer, pastoral care and manual labor alongside the poor; and Manning spent those two years of his life shoveling manure on nearby farms, washing dishes in a local restaurant, and building chicken coops. That is when Manning met Brother Dominique Voillaume.[4]

In one formative encounter when Manning had fallen into despair about his motives for entering the priesthood and this time of service with the Little Brothers, Voillaume had encouraged Manning with words that shaped Manning's spiritual trajectory from that day forward: "'You are on the threshold of receiving the greatest grace of your life. You are discovering what it means to be poor in spirit. Brother Brennan, it's okay not to be okay.'"[5]

---

3. Romans 9:21.

4. Manning, *All Is Grace*, 99–103.

5. For Manning, this saying became a life-long mantra of sorts for which Manning credits Voillaume. See ibid., 103.

It's okay not to be okay. This acceptance of our spiritual poverty before God precedes taking our hands off the controls. For Manning, Voillaume exemplified this daily giving over of one's life to God even in death— so much so that Voillaume was "a man who had surrendered, who had given pieces of his heart to others for a lifetime: a good word here, a gentle touch there, an encouragement always."[6]

When Voillaume learned he had inoperable cancer, he left the Little Brothers to return to Paris, where he took the graveyard shift as a night watchman in a factory. Every morning returning from work, Voillaume would visit the park across the street from his house, "an area filled with what society calls 'the riffraff': winos, the old and young and homeless, losers."[7] Manning writes:

> My good friend traded in his old habit for a new one, that of passing out candy to the least of these, listening to their stories, and always leaving them with good news, words I'd heard a hundred times: "Jesus Christ is crazy about you. He loves you just as you are, not as you should be."[8]

When Voillaume died, his journal was discovered, with this final entry:

> All that is not the love of God has no meaning for me. I can truthfully say that I have no interest in anything but the love of God which is in Christ Jesus. If God wants it to, my life will be useful through my word and witness. If He wants it to, my life will bear fruit through my prayers and sacrifices. But the usefulness of my life is His concern, not mine. It would be indecent of me to worry about that.[9]

My parents have always said I had a strong will growing up; by that I think they mean that obedience hasn't always come naturally to me. Calling the shots and dictating outcomes seems so much easier

6. Ibid., 106.
7. Ibid.
8. Ibid.
9. Ibid., 106–7

than saying to God on a daily basis, "Thy will be done," and then living as if I really meant those words.

And I venture to guess that a posture of total surrender to God is hard to come by for most of us. To approach life as if the only thing that actually mattered was the love of God working itself out in our relationships and in our tender acceptance of ourselves, warts and all? Up until now, that way of life has flat-out eluded me; still its inherent grace apprehends me, prodding me to embrace what can only be a gift from God to mere mortals.

Because when Jesus says he is the Way, and that "no one comes to the Father but through [him]," the invitation is to trust him and him alone to deliver us to our destination.[10] The invitation is to let Jesus fly the plane—and then to relax and breathe deeply, because we don't have to be the ones in charge anymore.

DISCUSSION QUESTIONS

1. Would you agree with Kristina's interpretation of "God is my co-pilot"? Why or why not?
2. Have you seen the bumper sticker, "God was my co-pilot, but we crashed in the mountains and I had to eat him"? Can you help Kristina understand what it means? Send your explanations to kristinarobbdover@gmail.com and she'll republish them at her blog, "Fellowship of Saints and Sinners."
3. What are some of the ways that we in our own lives try to take the controls from God?
4. When was the last time you tried to take the controls and fly the plane (metaphorically speaking)? How did that go for you?
5. When was the last time you gave the controls to God? How did it feel? What did you learn from the experience?
6. Why is it so hard to let go of needing to be in control when we can't be in control in the first place? What helps you let go?

---

10. John 14:6.

The Truth

Jesus answered, "I am . . . the Truth."
JOHN 14:26

7

I've Got Nothing Against God... It's His Fan Club I Can't Stand

Even though I'm a believer, I still find it really hard to be around other believers: they make me nervous, they make me twitch.

—BONO

I remain committed to Christ as always but not to being "Christian" or to being part of Christianity. It's simply impossible for me to "belong" to this quarrelsome, hostile, disputatious, and deservedly infamous group. For ten . . . years, I've tried. I've failed. I'm an outsider. My conscience will allow nothing else.

—ANNE RICE

The Truth

ONCE UPON A TIME, I found it easy to believe in the "holy, catholic and apostolic church."

That line from The Apostles' Creed that Christians in churches around the world recite every Sunday—"I believe in the holy, catholic and apostolic church"—I used to gloss right over without a second thought.

But that was before a vocation in ministry.

Nowadays, to mouth these same words requires a rather miraculous suspension of disbelief.

Because the sad reality I have experienced is that the church is rarely "holy," ("set apart" from the world in behavior), "catholic" (unified across denominational and cultural differences by God's Spirit), or "apostolic" ("sent out" into the world in God's cosmic mission of healing and restoration).

A church that is holy, catholic, and apostolic all at the same time? That would be harder to convince me of than the claim I had just won the lottery, when I've never once in my life bought a ticket! If there were ever a time in my past life when I held high expectations of the church, these have now been replaced by the modest wish that tomorrow I won't have to read yet another story in the news about the latest scandal.

The celebrity pastor who runs off with the church secretary or is caught with a gay prostitute.

The treasurer who absconds with church funds to pay for her luxury cruise.

The friendly, neighborhood priest convicted of child molestation.

The tiresome denominational squabbles and endless bickering and political infighting over everything from buildings, worship, and sex to what to wear on Sunday mornings.

If truth be told, the church is a complete and utter mess.

And this is a hard truth to tell. Many of us Christians would like to hide this reality from ourselves and one another, not to mention the rest of the world. Like a fraternity, we would prefer that those yet to be inducted into our ranks be protected from the big, embarrassing secret that the church is not really that different from the rest of the world, and that just because we claim to be God's "chosen people," we're not actually super-human. We still make mistakes, act terribly, treat one another shabbily, and harbor all kinds of weird hang-ups. Just about any aspiring television producer could package our dysfunctionality into yet another reality series: *Christians Behaving Badly* might not acheve higher ratings than the estrogen-exclusive alternative, *Girls Behaving Badly*, but would still qualify as popular entertainment.

But maybe in a world of illusions, the greatest gift the church can give the world is simply the truth about herself: that it is not because of any inherent goodness, achievement, or holiness of her own that the church exists to witness to God's love in and for the world. The church exists only because a sovereign God chose a community of people for himself, blessed them and then told them to go bless the world.

And the crazy, weird irony that makes some of us turn our backs on this way of being in community with God and with one another is the nature of what that so-called blessing looks like. Blessing Jesus's way is a revolutionary, topsy-turvy, counter-intuitive mode of looking at the world.[1]

"Blessed are the poor in spirit, for theirs is the kingdom of heaven," Jesus says about those who recognizes their deep need before God—when we might be quick to judge them as weak or dependent.

"Blessed are those who mourn, for they will be comforted," are Jesus's words of solace for those who grieve their own brokenness and this tragic world—while we might write them off as morose kill-joys.

"Blessed are the meek, for they will inherit the earth," Jesus promises those who have learned to still the violence of their own hearts in a world that rewards aggression and strife—when we would call them cowardly or powerless.

"Blessed are those who hunger and thirst for righteousness, for they will be filled," Jesus says about those who seek after God's goodness and justice—when we would dismiss them as naive idealists.

---

1. Matthew 5:3–12.

The Truth

"Blessed are the merciful, for they will be shown mercy," Jesus assures those who are slow to judge and quick to forgive—while we might view them as easily manipulated.

"Blessed are the pure in heart, for they will see God," Jesus reminds those who have made knowing God their single aim—when we would be tempted to see them as narrow-minded or simpletons.

"Blessed are the peacemakers, for they will be called children of God," is Jesus's reward for those who participate in the reconciling work of God in their lives and the world—when we might view them as Pollyannas.

"Blessed are those who are persecuted because of righteousness, for theirs is the kingdom of heaven; and blessed are you when people insult you, persecute you and falsely say all kinds of evil against you because of me," Jesus says about those who sacrifice their own comfort and life itself for him.

These sorts of blessings are probably not the kind most of us would quickly sign up for; but if being church means following Jesus together, then it also means learning to receive Jesus's blessings for ourselves, one another, and the world. To do this, I suspect, requires putting away hypocrisy: it asks us to stop trading in pat answers or cheap marketing gimmicks about how following Jesus has changed our lives overnight or made our lives easy, pain-free, successful, or even virtuous. It simply (and more profoundly) demands that we tell the truth about who we are and how Jesus has blessed us.

In his book *Messy: God Likes It That Way*, A. J. Swoboda shares an insight from more than twelve years of church planting and pastoring, which, in his own words, would have saved him "a ton of pain and heartache: lower your expectations of people and church."[2]

Swoboda goes on:

> When we idealize community, we idolize community. And when we idolize church and community, we forget the one who formed it. At the very place we make the church to be the club of the pretty people, we create and

---

2. Swoboda, *Messy*, 50.

imagine something that exists neither in reality nor in God's imagination.[3]

Swoboda, who pastors a new church community in Portland, Oregon, offers two alternatives to this bound-to-be disappointing, air-brushed picture of church: an Alcoholics Anonymous meeting where we all have really low expectations of those who show up, because everyone there is a mess-up; or, a great, big white elephant party.[4]

A white elephant exchange usually happens at Christmastime and becomes a prime opportunity to unload at least one piece of junk that has been sitting in your attic collecting dust: those ten-pound plate holders that you once bought in a fit of inspiration at the next-door neighbors' yard sale, maybe; or that ugly ceramic figurine with the cheesy, Hallmark inscription that a friend gave you and that you felt too guilty to throw away; maybe your old Debbie Gibson CD collection.

In developing the analogy, Swoboda describes one especially memorable white elephant exchange: "I decided that I would give away an old box of sensitive medical documents that I had saved over the years with information about my eye exams, vaccinations, blood tests, so on and so forth."[5]

He continues:

> I've been to lots of Christmas parties, and most of them are the same: karaoke, cookies with the little green sugar droppings, candy canes, and a really skinny Santa. None of them compared to this white elephant gift exchange. Imagine it. People fighting over the most useless stuff for the sake of fun. Everyone wanted my box of sensitive medical documents. My friend Dan has them today. I don't know if he has read them but if he ever does, I hope he still wants to be my friend. But what a blast. What a blast to make a gift out of some of your trash. A white elephant gift exchange is me seeing my trash in a new way, as a gift, as a contribution, as something of value.

3. Ibid.
4. Ibid., 49–50.
5. Ibid., 49.

What we think is trash becomes a gift. And that's what I think the church is. Some call it mass. I call it mess. Potatoes, potahtoes.[6]

The church is a community of people in which you and I can learn to see our crap as a gift for sharing.

The church is not where we pull out our fancy, expensive, name-brand possessions and show them off, as if to convince ourselves we are worthier or better off than the rest of the world. That would be to buy into a lie about the very nature of the church. That would be to fib about who we really are as a ragtag bunch of human beings called together because God loved us first.

Someone else before Swoboda articulated this same truth differently for his own time. When confronted by the specter of the German church's ugly collaboration with Adolf Hitler and the dictator's emerging "Final Solution," one German pastor and professor, Karl Barth, preached a sermon that reflected in places on the paradox of being the church:

> The church of Jesus Christ in the world—oh, what is it, this church? Must we not continually acknowledge that it is no different than any of those many other more or less good and hopeful human ventures? But especially full of sin and especially threatened because people are attempting something especially bold here: to proclaim the truth about the true God, to serve and worship this God! How could humankind in all its dubiousness and all its defenselessness emerge any more clearly than it does here? And how could this venture not continually be met by difficulties from the inside and from without? And how could this venture not secretly be afflicted, and in a particularly intense and severe way at certain moments in time such as the one in which we are now living? What remains of the church then? Where should it turn? What is to become of Jesus' disciples when they find themselves in exactly the same boat as the rest of humanity? They are no better off or stronger than the

---

6. Ibid., 50.

rest, no less lost and helpless than the world as a whole; indeed, more lost and helpless, perhaps, than all the rest.[7]

The church is "no better off or stronger than the rest, no less lost and helpless than the world as a whole; indeed, more lost and helpless, perhaps than all the rest"—this, from the leading Protestant theologian of the last century in the prime of his vocation.

Barth's words give voice to my own experience of trying to belong often restlessly to a dysfunctional family of people all gathered together because of a professed faith in Jesus Christ.

There truly are fewer things more preposterous than an indiscriminate assortment of human beings who have thrown in their lot with God himself and are trying, to differing degrees, to live like it. The whole project, in addition to being messy, is almost certainly bound for failure!

This is why any time the church pretends to be other than a bunch of screw-ups, it is doing violence to the gospel of Jesus Christ. Any time the church markets itself as an attractive, successful clique of people who have their act together and are worth your time on the basis of their good deeds or tidy lives, the church is putting Jesus up on a cross to crucify him one more time. To these sorts of people, Jesus actually says, "You have no part with me."[8]

Maybe a similar reasoning informs the Apostle Paul's determination to "know nothing" while he is with the Corinthian church "except Jesus Christ and him crucified."[9] Not Christ *and* the church. Not Christ and the latest church growth strategy. Not Christ and the latest three-year business plan or building project. Just Jesus Christ crucified.

In his first Letter to the Corinthians, Paul is writing to a fan club that is no less dysfunctional than it is today. Beset by rivalries and factions, the Corinthian church is justifying itself on its own merits as somehow more wise and more privileged than the rest of the world. Rather than preaching the crucified Jesus only, the

---

7. Barth, *The Word in This World*, 49.
8. John 13:8.
9. 1 Corinthians 2:2.

Corinthian church is preaching itself—and I can think of fewer things more diabolical.

Strikingly, Paul's message here is also not one of Christ crucified *and* Christ resurrected. The unadulterated message of "Christ crucified" rejects any triumphalism that the church has so often embraced. If in Jesus Christ we are "more than conquerors," as the Apostle Paul has said elsewhere, it is only because we stand beholding a cross upon which we, the church, have put our God to death over and over again.[10]

So, what does it mean to believe in the holy, catholic, and apostolic church, anyway? Does it mean we have to love and get along with God's fan club? Yes, I suspect—and *no*. Yes, to the degree that we recognize we're also one of God's annoying fan club and God loves us, regardless. Yes, insofar as we have appropriated God's topsy-turvy blessings for ourselves. Yes, if we are willing to share our white elephant presents with the rest of the gang.

But no, too . . . because if loving and getting along with God's fan club requires us to lie about ourselves, or to claim we're anything more than new creations and works in progress, struggling to follow along behind an often-elusive Jesus, then we have stopped believing in a church that is entirely an act of God, or a creation of Jesus Christ, or a work of the Spirit. And then we have pretended that that line in The Apostles' Creed is something other than an article of faith, by idolizing a church that is not holy, catholic, or apostolic.

DISCUSSION QUESTIONS

1. What kind of associations do you make when you hear the term, "God's fan club"? How do you react to this bumper sticker?

2. Based on your own experience, do you find it hard to believe in the "holy, catholic and apostolic church"? Why or why not?

3. How might the church (either your local church or the church in general) do a better job of telling the truth about itself and how

---

10. Romans 8:37.

God has blessed it?

4. *In what ways does the metaphor of church as a white elephant party or a meeting of Alcoholics Anonymous resonate with you? In what ways does it not?*

5. *How have you in your own life experienced the kind of blessings Jesus talks about in the Sermon on the Mount (Matthew 5–7)? Have you been able to share these with others? Why or why not?*

8

SHIT HAPPENS

Eat and drink together, talk and laugh together, enjoy life together; but never call it friendship until we have wept together.
—A traditional African saying

[God] causes his sun to rise on the evil and the good, and sends rain on the righteous and the unrighteous.
—Matthew 5:45

THE SUN WAS JUST rising above the thatched huts of our *tukuls* (mud huts) when I received my summons. All of the village elders had gathered, and I felt more embarrassed than honored that they would include me, the first *mzungu* (white person) to live in their midst, in this solemn, intimate assembly.

Shit Happens

We were there to pay our respects: the oldest matriarch in this little refugee compound at Uganda's northern border with Sudan had died during the night.

I knew very little about her.

Apparently, this ancient woman—no one really knew how old she was, but some insisted she was over one hundred—had lived out her twilight years as one of a few widows who, having lost their husbands to the war in Sudan, now cared for children orphaned by the war; and in recent months, she had been reduced to a lonely, bedridden existence, waiting for her end to come.

Only two nights before, I had been summoned at midnight to discuss what to do about the ancient woman's swift decline. In the crouching shadows cast by a small kerosene lamp against the walls of the little, round meeting hut where we had gathered, we had spoken in hushed tones about the options available; and, for a group of penniless refugees in a foreign land, the choices, like most resources, were scarce.

Should we borrow a car and hire a driver to take our patient to the hospital? we wondered. *Should we reevaluate her condition in the morning? Should we wait it out now and let her die in the comfort of her own home?*

We had rallied around the third option, and the woman had died the next day.

Now the woman's hut teemed with a crowd that sat huddled in somber silence. I was asked to offer a prayer, one which I stammered out uncomfortably, feeling like an interloper.

Soon we would gather in a long procession to carry the woman's body to a nearby field. The intermittent chorus of mournful wails rose as a priest, wearing the same tattered clerical collar he wore every day, intoned the words to an Anglican liturgy for the burial of the dead. The priest stood flanked by men swinging shovels, their sweaty bodies in the heat of the sun as dark as the mound of fresh dirt that had collected next to them.

As I watched the proceedings, something in particular struck me. This was a people who had seen unfathomable loss. The war in their homeland had killed nearly two million people and displaced another four million. Each of those present could testify to the very

The Truth

personal dimensions of this national tragedy. The stories they had told—of the loss of children, parents, spouses, and homes—had made me marvel at how these people could still wake up each morning to face another day. Yet somehow they could still come together with dignity and solemnity to grieve the death of a member of their community.

THE PROBLEM OF SUFFERING

The following summer, I had been in my *tukul* late one morning when the drone of a low-flying, Soviet-made Antonov bomber had sent us running for cover. Such frightening, real-life emergency drills had become routine, apparently, for my refugee friends. They had come to this displaced people's camp just across the border from their home country seeking protection from a ruthless regime's war on its own people, only to discover they were still vulnerable to these attacks.

The next day we visited the site where the plane had relieved itself of a heavy ball of nails and shrapnel just before making a clumsy U-turn in the sky like a great, sluggish bird, and heading north, back to where it came from. A woman came out to greet our small group of Westerners, which included a freelance photographer for *National Geographic*. We had come, we explained, to survey the damage and share the woman's story in churches back in America, to generate awareness and support on behalf of the plight of the South Sudanese people. The woman stood gesturing in animated tones to the large, crater-like hole in the ground just yards away from where her *tukul* stood. Fortunately, no one had been killed or injured, but a message had been sent.

Such horrors were not the only kind to greet my friends in their new place of so-called refuge. One day this same team of Westerners had visited another refugee compound even closer to the Sudan border. Our stay would be short. We had to leave before nightfall. That was when a lawless army of rebel soldiers known as "the Lord's Resistance Army" (LRA), led by a man named Joseph Kony, often raided these refugee villages, burning down infrastructure, stealing crops, and forcibly conscripting boys as soldiers and girls as concubines.

One of the women there told me about her nightly bedtime routine. When mothers elsewhere might be kissing their children's foreheads and tucking them under warm covers, bidding them "Sweet dreams," this mother would, with trembling limbs, hug her little ones, look upon them mournfully with the stark realization that she might never see them again, and then send them off to hide in the bushes for another anxious watch. This same mother told me she had stopped sleeping at night. Her story was just one of many that recounted the kind of trauma most of us will never see in our lifetimes.

As the shadows lengthened and our rickety pickup truck pulled out of that settlement, our hearts were heavily laden with the images and stories we had seen and heard in those few hours. I remember feeling guilty that we could leave while these new friends were stuck there. Their painfully felt physical immobility conveyed an even heavier psychological experience, which was an endless tunnel of trauma. If we could move on from what we had witnessed in that place, these people could not. Their lives would never be the same again. Ever.

And the latest breakthroughs in trauma theory would confirm this observation. Studies show that for many people who have experienced some traumatic event, like rape or war, for example, the trauma continues beyond the event itself, by way of recurring flashbacks, painful associations, and other emotional reenactments. Such affliction Oscar Wilde could describe as "one very long moment": "we cannot divide it by seasons. We can only record its moods, and chronicle their return. With us time itself does not progress. It revolves."[1]

Still, in the face of the worst suffering, my friends could somehow come together to weep and grieve over the comparatively less traumatic death of a nearly one-hundred-year-old woman. In fact, there was a sense in which all of this people's shared pain and grief had only strengthened the bonds of their community. My friends

---

1. Wilde, *De Profundis*, quoted in Parker, "Reliving Groundhog Day."

in that dreary refugee camp had seen a whole lot of senseless, unspeakable pain in their life, but somehow, they had also found deep connection and community in their suffering—so much so that the loss of one person to old age could draw a whole community's outpouring of support.

Shit happens. The really, really bad stuff—the suffering and the hurt—are just there. We're born into it and it belongs to our human condition. And this is a truth that the universe teaches and the Bible affirms. What we do with the shit—whether we let it alienate us or lead us into deeper solidarity with creation and our Creator, whether we let it become cause for despair or fodder for a deeper, more compassionate engagement with the world—is the crux, the cross, of the matter.

A LESSON IN PERSONAL LOSS

We ministers are assumed to be professionals at dealing with other people's troubles. Many of us have convinced ourselves that we are. We have equipped ourselves with the right pastoral and theological poopie scoopers for the fresh, steaming piles that we encounter on a regular basis.

I, too, have sat with many a person in their own, unique pain and listened to stories of heartbreak and loss. I, too, have stroked the foreheads of dying persons in their final hours and held the hands of loved ones as they grieve. I, too, have put in hours of clinical residency work just to learn how to be present to someone in their anguish without leaping to quick-fix solutions.

But suffering, by definition, quickly disarms the best-trained pros among us. Maybe this is because the very nature of suffering is that it shocks and bewilders us, burning away all those things we thought we knew about ourselves and our world. The conflagration can seem unbearably painful—not unlike a "fiery ordeal."[2] In one long moment, our preconceptions about the way the world works can go up in flames.

2. 1 Peter 4.

Shit Happens

A couple of years ago one of my dearest friends was diagnosed with ovarian cancer. She would die a little over a year later.

"I feel like a stranger on this street now," she had said one day while sitting on her porch and gesturing to her neighbors' homes, her head now bald due to an aggressive, weekly regimen of chemotherapy. She had lived on that same street for some twenty years. She and her husband had become fixtures of the neighborhood and pillars of the community. They had loved many people and earned the admiration and affection of many more.

As a hospice chaplain I had sat with many a dying patient before. I had beheld the daily plight of a refugee people and had shared in their grief. But for the first time I had been obliged to watch someone I knew well and loved suffer deeply and die; and, as I walked with my friend through her valley of death, praying with her, bringing meals, listening to her and crying with her, I gradually came undone.

Illusions die hard. Somehow I had tucked away the false assumption that my friend, by virtue of being one of the kindest, most caring people I knew, was immune to an untimely death; and, I had lived according to the unconscious mantra that if shit happens, it doesn't really happen to me and the people I most love—or at least, *not right now*.

Watching my friend gradually grow weaker and give up her fight shattered these illusions, and forced me again, this time in the context of personal loss, to come to terms with this basic bumper sticker truth: *shit really does just happen*. To everybody. Often senselessly. Often without any intrinsically redemptive reason.

"Shit happens" is a fact of life.

Which is why I need a God who has experienced the depth of our suffering and who stands in solidarity with us at the very site of our pain and grief.

I need a God who wears a cross.

I need a God who takes the work gloves off, rolls up his sleeves and, before we can protest, gets up to his elbows in stinky cow manure . . .

. . . Or, in paint. That was my dad putting on a fresh new layer of white paint on the walls of my dorm room at the start of my freshman year of college. The cheap, disposable, plastic roller we had received free of charge from the university had come apart in his hands, the latex paint virtually exploding onto his hands and clothes.

"See how much I love you?" he had exclaimed to his daughter, holding his paint-splattered hands out by way of emphasis.

I couldn't argue with him.

It is comforting to remember that when (not *if*) shit happens, and the metaphorical roller breaks, spilling paint all over us, God is with us; that when suffering threatens to undo us, God is there remaking us; that when pain, sin and brokenness bring us to tears, God is there weeping with us.

Thankfully, when God cries, a whole new world opens up. The cross is like a giant teardrop that waters the earth. Insofar as our tears are gathered up in the tears of God, they can water the parched places of this world and bring forth life.

And maybe it is in these places of our greatest suffering, rather than in the carefree stretches when all seems well with the world, that we are most capable of befriending this God who cries with us.

"Take up your cross and follow me," this God says.

Because there's solidarity to be found with God and with one another, right where it hurts.

DISCUSSION QUESTIONS

1. *What associations, if any, come to mind when you've encountered the bumper sticker, "Shit happens"?*

2. *What one personal experience has most taught you about the nature of suffering? What did you learn from it?*

3. *Does Jesus's death on the cross change how you view the crap in your life? If so, how?*

4. *How have you experienced God's nearness in times of pain and suffering? How have you not?*

5. *Kristina suspects that it is in the places of our greatest suffering that "we are most capable of befriending a God who weeps with us." What do you think about this statement, and why?*

9

Sex with my first boyfriend was a little bit like learning how to put in a tampon, but only half as enjoyable!

—Samantha Bee

I adjure you, O daughters of Jerusalem, by the gazelles or the wild does: do not stir up or awaken love until it is ready!

—One lover, Song of Songs

Focus on the Family cassette tapes playing the stern voice of James Dobson.[1] Scary videos with spooky, foreboding mu-

---

1. Evangelical author and politically prominent social conservative James Dobson founded the Christian organization Focus on the Family in 1977. In

sic and disturbing statistics about sexually transmitted diseases. Children's books about actual birds and bees. This bumper sticker evokes my earliest introductions to sex, which comprised a bewildering mix of swooning praise and fear-laden warnings. While I may never have been subjected to purity rings, as a child growing up in conservative evangelical circles, I still quickly inherited a host of conflicting emotions around this basic human activity.

At sixteen, to my parents' great horror, I chose as my first boyfriend a free spirit with dreadlocks who played the guitar, idolized Bob Marley, dreamt of hiking the Appalachian Trail in lieu of college, and like all teenage boys was on hormonal overdrive. Under the moonlight, next to a koi fish pond, all my girlish fantasies of a romantic, first kiss fell away with the aggressive darting movements of a teenaged boy's tongue in some primal rite of passage.

I wanted to run home and gargle.

That adolescent romance was short-lived: within weeks, the same boy who had stared dreamily into my eyes during surreptitious make-out sessions on his living room couch, and even braved meeting my parents over a mandatory dinner conversation—no, inquisition, met by awkward pauses and monosyllabic grunts—drove me home one night from the Homecoming dance only to shack up later that night with a girl who did not have a curfew and was willing to "go all the way."

A few mornings later he and I had broken up over the telephone, with me mustering as much tearful emotion as such an occasion seemed to call for, while all the while feeling surprised that I didn't feel more upset. Life would return to normal—later that afternoon—and, in hindsight, I was reluctantly grateful even at the time for parents who imposed a curfew, invited boyfriends to dinner, and insisted that "true love waits."

In college, when swimming teammates and sorority sisters spoke freely about their various hook-ups and one-night stands, I would listen vicariously to these revelations with a mixture of

---

the 1980s, at the time I was just beginning to learn about sex, Dobson was hailed as one of America's most influential spokespeople for social conservative causes. *Wikipedia*, s.v. "James Dobson," https//en.wikipedia.org/wiki/James_Dobson (accessed September 25, 2013).

curiosity, envy, and Schadenfreude. Before actor and comedian Mindy Kaling's resolution to agree that "hooking up = sex," because "everything else is 'made out,'" I was left to wonder at whether these one-time get-togethers really qualified as "going all the way."[2] At other times (when, for example, through the wall of my dorm room I could hear panting, euphoric exclamations to the tunes of a rickety bunk bed), I did not have to exercise my imagination.

Sex, imbued with an almost idolatrous mystique, was something I had learned was intended only for marriage. Falling short of this ideal seemed both tragic and, sadly, virtually unforgivable—even in the context of a committed relationship with a serious boyfriend who would later become my husband. I didn't realize it at the time, but in hindsight, I think I worshiped sex, and by extension marriage.

And with the passage of time, I have come to wonder whether we in many circles of the church have come to idolize this fundamental expression of our humanity. "True Love Waits," if once a commendable response to a sex-obsessed culture in which physical pleasure and immediate gratification are deemed of greatest value, has arguably only succeeded in making marriage and sexual purity false "promised lands" of sorts. In a stroke of irony, sexual abstinence campaigns have served to elevate sex in a different way—as some sort of heavenly transport for only the most so-called spiritual human beings among us who save ourselves for the conjugal bed.

For a young woman thrust into an intimidating world in which casual hook-ups and one-night stands seemed the prevailing norm for relationships, this admonition did spare me a lot of unnecessary pain and unwanted heartbreak; it also functioned as a kind of sinister warning laced with generous doses of guilt and shame, with the implication that whoever I gave my body and soul

---

2. Kaling writes: "There have been times when friends have said they hooked up with someone and all it means is that they had a highly anticipated kissing session. Other times it's a full-on, all-night, sex-a-thon. Can't we have a universal understanding of the term, once and for all? From now on, let's all agree that hooking up = sex. Everything else is 'made out.'" See Kaling, *Is Everyone Hanging Out Without Me? (And Other Concerns)*, 58.

to would *have* to be my husband, and anything less, a moral failure of the greatest sort.

In this sense, "True Love Waits" is, for me, a tried, tired, and loaded mantra . . . but is it fundamentally *true*? When stripped of its associations with a particular political agenda or the latest public morality campaign, can this statement belong to the Truth? Can it say something true about who God is in relation to human beings—something that will help us traverse this world of many competing and sometimes false loves?

SEX, LOVE, AND LIFE TOGETHER

If there isn't a bumper sticker yet, there should be for one theologian's understanding of erotic love: "coitus without co-existence is demonic," said the same Karl Barth who preached to a church cowed into submissiveness by Hitler's regime.[3] How's that for romantic sweet nothings of the kind you might whisper into a lover's ear?

But, more seriously, what Barth is getting at here is that sex is a fundamental expression of love between two whole people whose bodies and souls both belong to one other. In the same way that a person's sexuality represents one dimension of a whole, integrated self, sexual activity is one expression of love between two such persons. I suppose we lie to one another when we deny either the physical or spiritual component of this act, both of which are important. Maybe we also deceive ourselves when we pretend that sex somehow stands outside of the ordering of the rest of our life or of God's life in us.

If, for Barth, "co-existence" presumes marriage, marriage does not necessarily presume "co-existence." In other words, it would seem that Barth's challenge to two persons embarking on sexual union transcends easy categories of "married" or "unmarried," insofar as it asks any two persons considering a sexual relationship to answer the following questions for themselves, with a level of healthy fear and trembling:

3. Barth, *Church Dogmatics*, III/4, 133.

> What are you, you man and woman who are about to enter into sexual relations? What do you really want of each other? What is your business with each other? What have you in common? Is there any meaning in it? Is it demanded and sustained by your real life together? Is it justified and full of promise because at any rate you are honestly and resolutely on the way to achieving such fellowship?[4]

"True love," it seems, really does "wait" until such questions have answers—good ones. If it's easy to jump into the sack with someone, it's a whole lot harder to bare one's own soul. Real vulnerability with another human being requires far more than peeling off a couple layers of clothing. True intimacy is much riskier than showing someone else your naked body and a couple of love handles. Good sex is the byproduct of deep intimacy with another human being with whom we share all of life together as whole persons.

"True Love Waits" is also, I suspect, a more meaningful statement about a God who is *with* us. A God who in one creative burst of divine Eros makes us and then, like the proverbial distant clockmaker or the god of the theists, steps back to let us stumble along on our own, is not a God who desires to be in relationship with us—or *deserves* to be, for that matter. A God like that is not worthy of our love.

But in Jesus, "Immanuel," or, "God with us," God comes near and says, "I'm the One who has been with you all along and will be with you until the end."

In Jesus, God says, "I'm waiting, and I've got all the time in the world."

Now that's true love.

DISCUSSION QUESTIONS

1. *What are your associations with this bumper sticker? Do they resonate at all with your upbringing and earliest exposure to the topics of sex and sexuality? Why or why not?*

4. Ibid.

The Truth

2. Would you agree with Kristina's assessment of sexual abstinence campaigns—that where our culture has succeeded in idolizing sex (in terms of physical, immediate gratification) abstinence campaigns can succeed in idolizing sex in a different way (by hyper-spiritualizing it)? Why or why not?

3. How might Christians do a better job of conveying the gift and power of sex? Is Barth's statement, "Coitus without co-existence is demonic," helpful here? Why or why not?

4. How does a God who desires to be in intimate relationship with you and waits for you patiently to reach out to him change how you view yourself, your sexuality, and your relationships—or does it, for that matter? Why or why not?

10

The Next Time You Think You're Perfect, Try Walking On Water!!

"I think you have to try to fail, because failure gets you closer to what you're good at."
—Louis C.K.

"But we have this treasure in clay jars, so that it may be made clear that this extraordinary power belongs to God and does not come from us."
—2 Corinthians 4:7

A friend has said before, "Small people, small messes. Big people, big messes!"[1]

---

1. The succeeding passage about the Samaritan woman at the well has been republished with the permission of *Beliefnet*. See Kristina Robb-Dover, "Mess

The Truth

Have you ever wondered where God is in all of the mess?

One of my favorite stories from scripture is of the woman at the well.[2] If there were anyone who walked around with a great big sign on her forehead that reads, "I'm a mess," she would qualify. She has been through a string of dead-end relationships, each of them a failed experiment in love. When she comes to the well at midday all by herself, she is hot, tired, sweaty, and very much alone in her mess. She is probably one of many people, regardless of their circumstances, who walk around in a low-grade depression, disappointed by the way life has turned out.

Yet Jesus meets her there. Right in the middle of her mess He meets her. He doesn't wave a magic wand to make the mess go away or promise that he will be the one to clean it all up. He doesn't shrug off the mess as if it doesn't matter. He doesn't pretend that the mess is not there, either. (Have you ever been in a long conversation with someone only to discover in the mirror later that part of your lunch had been stuck to your face the whole time?)

If anything, Jesus may actually be the first person to tell this woman the honest-to-God truth—that she has been wearing a great, big sign on her forehead, or that the hummus sandwich she had at lunch splattered on her left cheek and is still there. Only Jesus doesn't use these words exactly. Instead he simply tells this woman what no stranger just passing through could ever guess without a direct connection to her soul: "You've had five husbands, and the man you now have is not your husband."

And then, if this woman with five husbands and a live-in lover can take the chance on another go at love, Jesus offers himself. "Living water," he calls his love that is true, as opposed to the same old, tainted water she has been drinking from other broken cisterns, which always leaves her thirstier than before. This water doesn't run dry like all those previous loves.

Does this woman's mess disappear after she meets Jesus? Maybe. Maybe not. The text won't say.

Happens," Fellowship of Saints and Sinners, *Beliefnet*, para. 1–12.

2. John 4.

What appears to change is the woman's ability to tell the truth about her mess. In the newfound light of how God sees her she can share her story freely without shame. She can acknowledge the mess that is there and the one who helped her face it while loving her all the same.

I used to think that the best indication as to whether Jesus had really met a person is how neat and tidy their lives appeared and how well they told their story about how Jesus had cleaned up their life (helped them get sober, healed them from sickness, turned their whole life around, and so on).

This story tells me otherwise: "The woman went back to the town and said to the people, 'Come, see a man who told me everything I ever did. Could this be the Christ?'"

No slick testimonies. No dogmatic apologetics. No pretenses that her life is all straightened out, or, even, that the stranger at the well is beyond doubt God himself. Only a willingness to be transparent about even her most embarrassing mistakes, and then an invitation to join in wondering along with her whether it really was God who just stopped by the local watering hole for a drink.

Why? Maybe because the person who has met Jesus is often the one walking around with the powdered sugar on her nose, or the toilet paper stuck to the sole of her shoe, who, once she realizes it can laugh—all because of the one who knew her through and through and loved her all the same. And, maybe this is the crux of a relationship with the only one who can actually walk on water: we don't have to pretend we're perfect; nor do we have to let our imperfections tell us who we are. We simply can share our story and point to where God shows up in it.

The funny thing is, God often shows up precisely in those places where we have gone to hide.

A woman with a checkered past comes to the well at midday to avoid the bustle of the afternoon happy hour, because she is hoping nobody will be there; and God shows up.

The prophet Elijah goes fleeing into the wilderness after a series of ministry mishaps leaves him depressed and depleted; there,

The Truth

in despair, he sits down and pleads with God to let him die; and God shows up.[3]

Adam and Eve cover themselves with fig leaves and slink away in shame, after disobeying God's order not to eat from the tree of the knowledge of good and evil; and God shows up.

"Where are you?" God calls out to them.[4]

The question elicits an honest answer.

When that same question visited me, I had to answer truthfully, too. The fig leaves—all of the various coping mechanisms I had relied on to hide my own brokenness—had worked for a time. I had managed to convince myself that I really could "walk on water"—be everything to everyone, perform flawlessly at all times, and fix all of life's messes.

Then one day I found myself standing in front of the mirror. A lifeless, vacant, hollow version of myself stared back. She seemed to be looking for me, wondering where I had gone. And then, either she or God himself, from the recesses of my own soul, whispered, "Where are you?"

And I answered truthfully, because grace is irresistible like that.

I was in a mess, too: my life seemed to be unraveling at the seams, and my perfectionism was only making matters worse.

"Where are you?" came the question.

I answered: "Here I am, God. Help me, please."

That was the moment I realized that perfectionism, if it doesn't kill you, can make you very sick.

THE BEAUTY OF IMPERFECTION

Epektasis is a fancy Greek word that sounds more like a venereal disease than a theological concept. The fourth-century theologian Gregory of Nyssa actually coined the term as a way of reframing the nature of true perfection in the spiritual life.[5] True perfection,

3. 1 Kings 19.
4. Genesis 3:8–13.
5. Gregory of Nyssa, *The Life of Moses*, 5;131–32.

for Gregory, consisted not in reaching some elusive end of contented bliss, at which point one had perceived everything there was to know about God and had attained completion of character. To arrive in this sense would mean an end to the adventure of learning and discovery. It would render one the spiritual equivalent of a couch potato endlessly feasting on seven-layer dip.

Instead, perfection a là Gregory takes shape in the journey itself—a journey into the life of God that continues incessantly after death—so that imperfection becomes a positive, life-affirming space in which to receive God's grace, rather than an Achilles' heel to hide or cover. Those prickly imperfections we recognize in ourselves and others? Our deficiencies or disabilities? They become apertures through which God's grace slips in; points of communion with God and with one another; the creative material by which God is fashioning us more and more into who we were meant to be from the very beginning.

In this context, "perfectionism" (as a striving for flawlessness) is little more than a diabolical, life-sucking lie we tell ourselves: it is like saying we really can "walk on water" and don't need God's help to do it, when in fact, the water is steadily rising above our head.

Anne Lamott says this well in her book, *Bird by Bird: Some Instructions on Writing and Life*:

> Perfectionism is the voice of the oppressor . . . It will keep you cramped and insane your whole life, and it is the main obstacle between you and a shitty first draft. I think perfectionism is based on the obsessive belief that if you run carefully enough, hitting each stepping-stone just right, you won't have to die. The truth is that you will die anyway and that a lot of people who aren't even looking at their feet are going to do a whole lot better than you, and have a lot more fun while they're doing it.[6]

Perfectionists ultimately suffer from an inability to accept the truth that God loves them *apart* from their achievements—that "while we were still sinners, Christ died for us."[7] Perfectionists need a

---

6. Lamott, *Bird by Bird*, 28.
7. Romans 5:8.

divine intervention, or, in my case, a gradual exorcism. We need a clear-eyed Jesus and a small community of close friends to tell us lovingly and matter-of-factly the truth about ourselves—that no matter how hard we might try, we cannot earn the love of God on our own merits, and that for our own good, we need to stop trying.

EMBRACING OUR IMPERFECTIONS

When my daughter, Sam, was diagnosed several years ago with developmental delays, I found myself asking why.[8] In those first days of Sam's initial diagnosis by a pediatric neurologist, followed by a host of medical tests, and in turn, weekly therapy interventions in the years to come, I was often reminded of the story of the blind man in the Gospel of John.[9]

"Who sinned, this man or his parents, that he was born blind?" the disciples ask Jesus, seeking some sort of explanation.

Neither, Jesus answered. The man was born blind "so that God might be glorified." On my darker days I am inclined to wonder why God demands so much glory.

When Sam was seventeen months and still had yet even to crawl, not to mention walk or run the way other kids her age were doing with ease, I had finally heeded my intuition that something was wrong and taken her to a physical therapist. At the time Sam would happily scoot on her behind anywhere and everywhere with little concern for a developmental index that put her near the bottom of a bell curve and gestured to some underlying condition.

In the days and weeks to come, we would do tests and more tests; Sam would work with a physical therapist to learn how to walk; and, when Sam finally did walk, her first steps elicited great celebration. (There had been a time when even walking was not a guarantee.) In due time, we would discover Sam also needed speech therapy and occupational therapy even as her condition would

---

8. The reflections that follow have been republished with the permission of *Patheos*. See Kristina Robb-Dover, "Blessed Imperfection: A Girl Learns To Walk, and Her Mother, To Take Her First Steps," in Amy Julia Becker, "Thin Places," *Patheos*, para. 1–21.

9. John 9.

remain a medical mystery. The closest we had gotten to a diagnosis was one neurologist's scary catch-all term for anything that did not yet have a name: "cerebral palsy," she had said to me one day matter-of-factly in the examining room, as if she were remarking on the day's weather.

Time seemed to stand still in that moment.

But Sam was also the baby girl whose movements on a sonogram during the eighth month of pregnancy looked like dancing, causing the doctor to burst out in exclamation that "Your daughter is an unusually happy little girl!" Sam was the child whose smile lit up a room and still does. Hers was the pregnancy that sent me to the drive-through at the local McDonalds every morning during the worst weeks of morning sickness—all for an Egg McMuffin, the only thing that could stave off the nausea. She was the one who, days before a pregnancy test could have produced accurate results, was announced as a Christmas present by her future godmother, a woman reputed for her gifts of prophecy in the congregation I served as a minister; and, Sam was the one for whom I clung tenuously to that same prophecy, "God's Word will not return to Him empty," when a blood clot near Sam's head during the first months of pregnancy threatened miscarriage.[10]

Later, in her toddler years, when other children her age had by now mastered walking, and were running, climbing steps, and even jumping off ledges, Sam was the one who would sit quietly and contentedly reading her books, or scoot clumsily along on her behind. She, in her unruffled satisfaction, could have cared less about some developmental index that put her near the bottom of a bell curve, even if it pained her mother.

When at three-and-a-half, she could not yet jump off a one-foot step, Sam and I would stand on any landing we could find practicing. I would hold Sam's hands, coaxing, cajoling, and cheering Sam on to jump, my inner anxieties mounting with each failed attempt, my efforts at patience faltering—no matter that my daughter's brain could not locate the right neuromuscular command required for the task at hand.

10. Isaiah 55:11.

The Truth

One day these efforts had landed us on the steps in front of our local library, Sam's favorite place. (If she could, my daughter would spend hours in the "wibrary" just plowing through the books, immersed in the pictures.) We were standing on the bottom step and my daughter's brain could not tell her to jump, despite her efforts to do so and my increasingly frantic efforts to urge her do so. And the more frustrated Sam could sense I was becoming, the more unwilling she was to consider this enterprise fun or worth her time. With each failed attempt to lift both her legs off the ground and jump up and forward, her left foot would fall limply on the ground and Sam would grin with the satisfaction of one who had done her best and followed the instructions, only to look into a mother's face registering a mix of anxiety and discouragement.

In times like these, God's best gifts for me are often the hardest to receive. Sam's challenges are the perfect gift for a mommy who has lived her life according to some unwritten rule that perfection consists in achievement and excellence in high performance. When my own impatience meets Sam's challenges, it is as if God is gently prying me free yet again from the illusion that I am superhuman.

Why, after all, in a world of one God and one God alone, would we want to be anything but simply and perfectly human?

My daughter is perfect (perfectly human, that is) not because she could jump gracefully off a one-foot step by the age of two. Or pronounce her sentences correctly. Or, at four years of age, finally poop in the potty.

My daughter is perfectly human not because she was made in my *own* image or succeeds in rising to all my own ridiculously high bars for "success." Beauty. Smarts. Physical grace. Moral goodness. (My internal list, I am discovering, is immensely long and impossible to fill.)

Sam is perfectly human, because she was made in *God's* image, and because she is being who God made her to be: a happy, carefree, beautiful little girl with a deep compassion for others and a capacity to love that calls others out of themselves.

A friend remarked to me, "Every child is a special needs child."

I agreed, then added, chuckling, "And every adult is a special needs adult, too."

Sam's special needs have made me painfully more aware of my own. Her challenges are mine not just because I am her mother, but because God is using her growing edges to illuminate my own more hidden but arguably more serious imperfections. Pride. Impatience. An illusion of self-sufficiency. A need to dictate outcomes and be in control. These are the rough edges that God is sandpapering.

For this I can only be grateful—grateful to be human and happy to be imperfect. I have a long way to go, and that's a good thing; because if recognizing and apprehending wholeness demands an experience of being broken, then the brokenness need no longer seem quite so paralyzing or scary in the first place.

For the longest time I did not understand Jesus's meaning when he instructs the disciples to "be perfect as your Heavenly Father is perfect."[11] I can appreciate the sentiments here of author Amy Julia Becker, who was obliged to reassess her definition of human perfection upon the birth of a daughter with Down Syndrome. I, like Becker, once mistook human perfection for "exceptionalism."[12] Excellence at anything and everything, be it mastery of academics or sports or parenting or ministry. This misconception probably at least unconsciously shaped the first half of my life, much of which was spent running a fast-paced performance treadmill.

But Becker points out that the word for "perfection" in the original Greek here is *telos*, meaning "that for which you were intended."[13] In other words, "perfection" is doing that for which you were made to do—becoming who you were meant to be as a person, made in God's image. In this sense, perfection aligns with how God made you—your true self.

Catholic theologian Hans Urs Von Balthasar has offered a perspective not unlike that of Gregory of Nyssa: "perfection consists in fullness of [life's] journey," he has written. None of us must ever think we have "arrived."[14] Each day with Sam reminds me I have a long way to go in becoming my true self; and, if my journey seems

---

11. Matthew 5:48.
12. Becker, "About," *Thin Places*, para. 5.
13. Ibid.
14. Balthasar, *Heart of the World*, 23.

incomplete, it is only because the fullness of a life well-lived still beckons me. Love, joy, peace, patience, kindness, goodness, faithfulness, gentleness, and self-control: these "fruit of the Spirit" that will overflow out of a life fully lived so often elude me as I seek to be who God made me as Sam's mother and as a child of God; but when they do, they call me back to the journey itself, as reminders of the grace before me.

And if the road ahead is long, it is so because God's love is longer—and deeper and wider—than our own little heads and hearts could ever imagine or comprehend. If the journey is incomplete, it is so because there is so much fullness to be had. To "arrive" would be to stop learning—maybe even to stop truly loving. In this sense, I am grateful the journey will never end.

DISCUSSION QUESTIONS

1. *Have you struggled with perfectionism? Or, to phrase it another way, when did you last try walking on water and how did it go? What did you learn in the process?*

2. *What are your biggest imperfections? What failures or mistakes are you most ashamed about? How, if at all, have you sought to hide them?*

3. *How have you typically defined perfection?*

4. *What do you make of Gregory of Nyssa's concept of "epektasis" (that perfection consists in the journeying itself)? How, if at all, does this reframing of perfection change how you look at your imperfections?*

5. *Where would you most like to see God free you from the pretense that you can fix the mess, either in your life or in the lives of others?*

6. *Kristina shares the story of the Samaritan woman as an example of what can transpire when God meets us in our messes. Are there other stories from scripture that come to mind as examples?*

The Next Time You Think You're Perfect, Try Walking on Water!!

7. When was the last time that God met you in your failures and imperfections? What happened? How did the experience change you?

11

Visualize Whirled Peas

> *If you're a woman and a guy's ever said anything romantic to you, he just left off the second part that would have made you sick if you could have heard it.*
> —Louis C.K.

> *The movement from naïve optimism to cynicism is the new American journey.*
> —Paul E. Miller

My daughter as a baby hated whirled peas. That unnaturally green purée was understandably unpalatable, and I used every method of parental persuasion available.

Spoons that became an airplane; feigned delight while forcing down a bit myself; promises of ice cream when the peas were done. None of these tactics proved particularly convincing.

Somewhere along the way I stopped buying whirled peas at the grocery store.

"Gerber's baby food" was a common answer when I asked Facebook friends what came to mind when they see this bumper sticker.

"Whirled peas" might also mean:

- "Pea-green goo swirling hypnotically. Maybe in Scooby Doo-like animation."
- "Hippies."
- Vegetative peace, in the form of "giant peas wearing flags/colors representing their country," or its polar opposite: "giant peas wielding swords."
- And, from a scholar-philosopher in our midst: "the exhaustion of a phrase playing on an exhausted phrase."

Whenever I see this bumper sticker, I am reminded that the airy idealism of one of our finest aspirations deserves some tongue in cheek ribbing; and, that we live in a world of illusions where people and things are rarely what they seem. "Whirled peas" sounds like "world peace" but sure as heck is not the same thing. Something similar could be said of so many things in this life that on the surface may appear to be one thing but are actually another.

In his days of comedy clubs, Woody Allen used to do a stand-up routine about a time when he was down south and was invited to a costume party:

> And you have to get the picture: I'm walking down the street in a deep southern town; I have a white sheet over my head. And a car pulls up and three guys with white sheets say, "Get in." So I figure they're guys going to the party . . . as ghosts, and I get into the car, and I see we're not going to the party, and I tell them. They say, "Well, we have to go pick up the Grand Dragon." All of a sudden it hits me . . . down south, white sheets, the Grand Dragon . . . I put two and two together: I figure there's a guy going

The Truth

to the party dressed as a dragon. All of a sudden a big guy enters the car, and I'm sitting there between four clansmen, four big-armed men, and the door's locked, and I'm petrified, I'm trying to pass desperately, y'know, I'm saying "Y'all" and "Grits," y'know, I must have said "grits" fifty times, y'know. They ask me a question, and I say "Oh, grits, grits." And next to me is the leader and you can tell he's the leader, cause he's the one wearing contour sheets, y'know...[1]

In the end Allen manages to elude those three clansmen and a death by hanging, by giving a stirring speech about how "this country can't survive unless we love one another, regardless of race, creed, or color.... "And they were so moved by my words, not only did they cut me down and let me go, but that night, I sold them two thousand dollars worth of Israel Bonds," Allen jokes.

In a world of untrustworthy appearances and misleading first impressions, disillusionment is simply inevitable, and cynicism? Cynicism is only a short, leisurely stroll from disillusionment... or, a ride in a car with three sheet-clad members of the Ku Klux Klan.

In fact I would venture to guess that it is hard not to grow at least a bit jaded in a world like ours. A world in which our highest ideals have become tired clichés; in which our finest institutions, including the church, have proved to be as deeply flawed as they are necessary; in which the people whose integrity we have put our trust in often fail us; in which even our loves can now be "virtual." The reality is that much can conspire to make us cynical.[2] We can become distrustful of those things that seek to captivate us or claim our allegiance in some way. We can wonder if they are "too good to be true," or roll our eyes when they prove false.

The stirring and persuasive rhetoric of politicians in the wake of yet another national tragedy may quickly ring hollow when

---

1. Allen, "Down South," *Woody Allen Standup Comic*.
2. In January 2013 headlines about a certain college athlete who had fallen in love with someone he had never met and had only virtually corresponded with captured international interest when it turned out the person who was supposedly his girlfriend didn't really exist.

succeeded by a mealy-mouthed, watered-down bill representing only the interests of our nation's deep-pocketed lobbyists.

Whirled peas.

Or the dream job that sounded glamorous and exciting may turn out to be menial, boring, and soul-destroying.

Whirled peas.

Or the prescription pill that promises TV viewers suffering from insomnia or a poor libido a peaceful night's sleep or an exhilarating sex life, may come with a long list of precautionary directions regarding use, including warnings of serious liver damage, cancer, and even death.

Whirled peas.

Or the man who looks the part of a Christian ethicist at an Ivy League university may actually be a congenital liar and philanderer. He may speak with gravitas at all those academic conferences about lovely praiseworthy ideals, and sound like he means what he says; he may even drive a Saab, sport a designer watch, and on occasion wear black turtlenecks with his blazers. But underneath it all, even that designer watch is probably a knock-off.

Whirled peas.

THE GIFT OF CYNICISM

Writer Addie Zierman, creator of the blog *How To Talk Evangelical*, says the day she understood her cynicism was the day she heard her son's heartbeat.[3] She was lying on a doctor's examining table when the understanding came: "I heard that wild, beating heart, and I wanted more than anything to protect it from all of the sharp things in the world," Zierman writes.[4] "And all at once, it occurred to me that *I* had become one of those things—sharp and angry. Hardened and removed. I was sitting arms crossed, at the edge of things, daring those Church People to impress me. I was looking at the world with narrowed eyes, and all I could see was the cracks."[5]

3. Addie Zierman, "Making Your Faith Your Own," para. 1–4.
4. Ibid.
5. Ibid.

The Truth

Zierman recalls that she didn't want to stay in that state forever. She wanted to be a soft and gentle outlet for her son.[6] Still, she could later remember that cynicism as a gift of sorts (my words not hers). It was a gift insofar as it helped her stare down the various bogeymen that confronted her, like pain, brokenness, darkness, and religious hypocrisy. It was a gift to the degree that it moved her from the shallows of easy answers that paper over the unexplainable, inherently tragic dimensions of life, to the depths of a faith that had weathered dark storms and ultimately prevailed. That cynicism was a gift, because it ultimately belonged to a process of authenticating Zierman's faith as hers and nobody else's.[7]

"The moment when faith really 'becomes your own' happens after you have seen the whole God thing for all of its uncertainty, all of its hardness, all of its pain and brokenness and hypocrisy . . . and choose it anyway," Zierman writes.[8]

My own sharp things have come with time and a few hard knocks: sometimes I have wanted to hide them, so as to fit in with a happier-go-luckier version of evangelical Christianity—the kind evoked by the sparkly-white, teethy grins of popular televangelists who tell me all I really need are more positive thoughts. Nowadays I'm learning to see these same jagged edges—ones that for many years I hid with a smile—as the makings of a faith that is truly and uniquely my own. Cynicism need not be only a measure of past wounds or a means of self-preservation from future ones (although it is unapologetically this, too). It can give way to a more robust, personally tested belief in Christ, one shorn of its childish, Pollyanish attachments.

---

6. Ibid., para. 6–7.

7. Here is Zierman in her own words: "One Big Thing happens to us or a lot of things happen, one after another. And then there's this moment of stunning clarity, and we see that everything that we once thought was so entirely perfect is cracked to its deepest heart. And listen: *this is good.* This is such an important moment, and without it, we'd spend our whole lives swimming in some man-made lake instead of the Living Deep." Ibid., para. 11–16.

8. Ibid.

BEYOND CYNICISM

I have to believe that whoever wrote Psalm 116 (probably King David) was at one time or another a cynic, or at least subject to dramatic mood swings. The funny thing is, that Psalm is one of the "Hallelujah" or "Praise" songs. The song earns this classification because it begins and ends by praising God.

But interspersing the Psalm's exclamations of worship are dramatic admissions of just how jaded the Psalmist had become by the time God rescued him: "The snares of death encompassed me; the pangs of Sheol laid hold on me; I suffered distress and anguish . . . I said in my consternation, 'Everyone is a liar.'"[9]

I said in my consternation, everyone is a liar. (During my chaplain residency at a hospital, I met people in visits to the psych unit who made similar remarks.) But there is something profound at play here. The Psalmist is saying that when he had become so cynical he could no longer trust the motives of anyone, the trustworthiness of God breathtakingly apprehended him. God was credible when no one else was; God was reliable, trustworthy and true all the way to hell and back.

There is a sense in which the Psalmist's expression of cynicism serves to illuminate and bring into full relief the unchanging dependability of God's love. Sometimes we need to be painfully wrenched free of our illusions, so much so that we find ourselves "consternated," jaded, and angrily cynical, before we can truly appreciate the depth of God's constant reaching out to us. And, because the grace of God can trump the cynicism of the most jaded among us, even cynicism can find a place in our praise.

Maybe it is because Jesus knew we would have many attachments, many of which would let us down, that Jesus says, "Abide in me."[10] "I am the Vine; you are the branches." Jesus is contending that when all of our other commitments, convictions, and allegiances will let us down or be potentially burned up in the fire of living and dying—in that great, big furnace of the Truth—we will be glad we

---

9. Psalm 116.
10. John 15:5.

stuck close to the one, True Vine. Jesus is true and trustworthy like nothing or no one else.

Which is not to imply, on the one hand, that such attachments or allegiances are not themselves good or worthy of pursuit or devotion, or, on the other, that they warrant total complacence or disengagement, which might be a more natural, tragic extension of cynicism. These attachments simply aren't *the* Truth that is also the Way and the Life: they can only take us so far into that spacious mansion with many rooms where God dwells in us and we in God, where all the world is finally and completely set right with its Maker.[11] Only the one who is the Way, the Truth and the Life can do this. Only the one whose Story all our own smaller, incomplete truths inhabit—like cramped servants' quarters in a magical, ginormous castle with unending rooms—can lead us there.

And somewhere there, in that mansion with many rooms, it is possible that even our cynicism will find a drawer in which to lie. Maybe every so often we'll rediscover it, dust it off, and try it on again—much like that old Varsity Letterman jacket we used to wear in high school, now packed away in a storage trunk smelling of mothballs. If we once wore that white, leather jacket with pride, secretly relishing its green lettering and the statement it made about our athleticism, now we have no use for it: we may even find it a bit childish and silly. But maybe we will want to hold on to it, anyway—if only for a good laugh and the reminder of how far we've come.

DISCUSSION QUESTIONS

1. What comes to mind when you visualize "whirled peas"? What comes to mind when you visualize "world peace"?

2. How would you define cynicism? Would you agree with Kristina's definition of cynicism as a general distrust or suspicion of those things that seek to captivate us or claim our allegiance in some way?

3. Would you agree with Addie Zierman and Kristina that

---

11. John 14:12.

cynicism can be a gift? Why or why not?

4. Do you think young people today are by and large more cynical than they were, say, fifty or one hundred years ago? Why or why not?
5. When was the last time that a person or ideal let you down, and what did you learn from the experience?
6. What sorts of things do you find easiest to be cynical about and why?
7. How might Jesus's self-description as "the Truth" challenge or redirect our cynicism?

The Life

Jesus answered, "I am . . . the Life."
JOHN 14:26

12

> *When Jesus said "Love your enemies," I think He probably meant don't kill them.*
> —Another popular bumper sticker in my neighborhood

> *I just want to say, you know, "Can we all just get along?"*
> —Rodney King, in the wake of the 1992 Los Angeles riots

These days I see this sticker and its variations just about everywhere in my downtown Atlanta neighborhood. There is the "C" paired with the crescent star representing Islam. The peace symbol.

The Life

An "e" with the scientific symbols for male and female. The star of David for Judaism. An "i" topped by another little star (this one for the pagan-Wiccan faith). An "s" circumscribed by the Buddhist yin and yang. Then, finally, a "t" in the shape of the cross signifying the Christian faith.

The Polish artist, Pyotr Mlodozeniec, originally designed the "Coexist" image in 2001 as a way to promote religious tolerance, but the image's popularity only really skyrocketed several years later, after Irish rock band U2 made use of the graphic in their 2004 worldwide "Vertigo Tour."

What does it really mean to coexist? Is it a reminder of the lessons we learned in kindergarten—lessons about the importance of being kind and sharing? Is it an inspirational call to embrace world peace and good will between all peoples? Is it a summons to mushy relativism?

Maybe coexistence is about something even more basic to human life. Coexistence doesn't require too much of us, after all: it only asks that we let one another be (which can be as simple as leaving one another well enough alone); and, that we find ways to stop killing one another.

If this sticker calls for anything more demanding, it is only that we find ways to live alongside one another, if not exactly together. That we respect one another's differences. That we tolerate one another—maybe as we would a roommate who leaves dirty dishes in the sink or a spouse who snores.

In a day and age when suicide bombers blow up innocent people and religious fundamentalists picket funerals with hateful slogans, to "coexist" is to get along well enough that we, the human race, refrain from going extinct. And this preservation is no small thing.

In his book *Near Occasions of Grace*, the Franciscan contemplative Richard Rohr, quoting psychotherapist Adele Getty, makes the following observation about the times in which we live: "Rather than confront the social, political, and spiritual dilemma of the day, human growth has become a pacifier, the means to avoid the larger issues of human survival."[1] Rohr goes on to note that today "it may be acceptable to repress the objective issues of famine, destruction of habitat, medical care, and arms sales to everybody, but it is a mortal sin to repress any feelings, fears, or sexual fantasies."[2]

To coexist is to find ways to survive together in the face of those things that would threaten to undo us. To learn how to get along, yes. But also to recognize and uphold our common living space and shared fate as human beings.

Some Christians find this statement infuriating. They see it as the very antithesis of Christ's call to "go and make disciples."[3] Jesus, they say, was not content to let people be just as they are. He came to overturn an unjust order of haves and have-nots and to show us a new way of living that makes a nonsense of mere coexistence, with the result that we Christians have much better news to put on our cars than merely, "Coexist." The implication? That we Christians are our brothers' and sisters' keepers. That the well-being and eternal fate of our Muslim neighbor, Buddhist friend, or spiritual-but-not-religious colleague are necessarily our business.

And while there is truth in this view, this perspective can miss out on something much more fundamentally and intrinsically important about God's grace. Because the Bible affirms, before anything else, that in the beginning God created human beings and called us good; and that we, each of us, have been made in God's image, and that this same God who created us out of love also sustains us, so that in God we "live, move and have our being."[4]

In other words, it is because of God and God's life in each of us, regardless of who we are or where we come from or what we believe, that we are able to breathe, or eat, or run, or dance. Such things are gracious displays of God's provision and examples of what Christians have sometimes called "prevenient grace." They signify God's love for all creation, a love that does not depend on

---

1. Rohr, *Near Occasions of Grace*, 12. By "human growth," Rohr takes Getty to mean (and I am paraphrasing) self-development on a therapist's couch.
2. Ibid.
3. Matthew 28:19.
4. Acts 17:24.

our decision for or against Christ. They are the gracious marks of simply being alive and of God's delight in us just the way we are.

When we try to impose our views or way of life on another human being, or when we suppose that it is ultimately up to us to convert our neighbor, then we can actually get in the way of God's prevenient grace. I suppose in fact we come close to denying it, both for our neighbor and for ourselves. Who ever said that God's love depended on *us*, anyway? On *our* intelligence or inherent goodness or persuasiveness? Who, for that matter, ever said that God's love depended on our neighbor accepting what we believe in its entirety?

Grace, by definition, is unconditional.

Have you ever been lectured by someone who believed so strongly in something that they tried to convince you that their way of doing things or their approach to God was unquestionably, unassailably right? Have you ever *been* that person? If so, then you know what I'm talking about when I say that it is often harder to befriend someone without requiring that they change how they live to meet our standards. In our anxiety we can feel like it is our duty to deliver enlightenment or salvation to others, or, that our experience of reality has to be normative for someone else in order for it to be valid for ourselves.

I remember visiting a church service once to find that I was the only one in the group unable to speak in tongues. Some in the group were falling down "slain in the Spirit," as the expression goes.[5] Others were jumping up and down, or ecstatically waving their hands praising Jesus, speaking in indistinguishable, rapid-fire syllables.

I must have stuck out like a Christmas caroler at a Jewish celebration of Passover, because at some point in the proceedings the pastor came and laid his hands on my head and prayed for God to give me the gift of tongues. I remember feeling in those moments a bit like Steve Carrell's character, Michael Scott, in one episode of the hit TV series *The Office*: as the regional manager for the paper

---

5. The expression "slain in the Spirit" is more prevalent in Charismatic and Pentecostal Christian circles. It suggests not an actual death but a state of being so overcome by an encounter with the Holy Spirit that one falls down on the ground.

company Dunder Mifflin, Michael discovers he is the last to know the latest, juicy subject of office gossip. An uninitiated Michael, feeling insecure and left out, does his best to get up to speed on the rumors by circulating some of his own.

If this church service was a spiritual fraternity, then I was at rush. Here was the moment of reckoning when I would discover if I measured up as spiritually fit enough to qualify for admission. Maybe I could have refused that pastor's laying on of hands and ensuing prayer, but if truth be told, the Michael Scott in me wanted to be in the know, to acquire all the marks of belonging.

And I would be lying if I said I wasn't tempted to pretend. To spout out some indiscernible form of pidgin language and fall on the ground in a dramatic show of spiritual anointing. To exclaim loudly, "Thank you, Jesus, for giving me the gift of tongues!" so that I could belong—or, at least, be less an object of religious pity in that suddenly suffocatingly small room.

The truth also is that when that pastor prayed, nothing happened—nothing, that is, that made me sound like the rest of the bunch.

Some years later, during a difficult time in my life, God would give me this special prayer language of tongues to use in private times of pouring out my heart to God—in this sense, maybe God answered that pastor's prayer—but not then. Not in those moments. In those moments I felt just awkward and out of place.

Do you think I ever darkened the door of that church building again?

YOU ARE ACCEPTED

It is hard to let people simply be as they are when we would prefer to make them like ourselves, in our own image. It is equally hard to be that one person others are trying to change. But maybe the hardest thing to do is to accept that God himself lets us be just as we are, without forcing himself on us—even as God constantly reaches out to us.

The Life

Scripture says that "no one has ever seen God."[6] Even the Old Testament spiritual heavyweight, Moses, who climbs Mount Sinai to commune with God before receiving the Ten Commandments, has to be content with a view of God's backside. Why? Because if he were to see God face to face he would not be able to live.[7] A face-to-face encounter with God would be too much for him: it would kill him.

God chooses to let us live.

The Bible claims that the closest representation we have of God—precisely because he is God in the flesh—is the person of Jesus Christ. And this Jesus is *with* people. He is with people where they are. Sure, he tells them the truth about themselves. Sure, he at times points people in a particular direction—towards truth, or healing, or forgiveness, or love of God and neighbor; towards "Living Water" for the Samaritan woman at the well, or towards spiritual rebirth for the jaded religious teacher Nicodemus.

But Jesus also never imposes his way on his interlocutors or on us, when he could. He simply is there in the messiness of real lives, all the while holding out endless possibilities for new and abundant life. And, the God who sends his only Son, "so that whoever believes in Him might have eternal life," is also the same God who opens the door to where that life is.[8] God has an open-door policy.

God coexists with us.

Even when we would prefer to put God to death over and over again, on a cross and in all manner of ways when we tell God we don't need God, or would prefer that God would get lost, or pretend God is not there, God keeps on holding out life to us all the same. And all the while God lets us be just as we are, even as God offers more life-giving goodness.

Because in the same way that God called us "good" at creation, God in Jesus Christ keeps on calling us worthy of being alive long after we blow it and keep on blowing it.

---

6. John 1:18.
7. Exodus 33:20–23.
8. John 3:16.

Long after we fail to coexist with the self we once knew, God is still there.

The more I think about it, it is a miracle, really, that after all these years of existing and failing to coexist the human race hasn't destroyed itself in any manner of ways.

I guess God has an exceptionally high level of tolerance.

DISCUSSION QUESTIONS

1. *How do you react when you see this bumper sticker? What kind of people do you typically associate with this bumper sticker?*
2. *Do you agree or disagree with Kristina's definition of what it means to coexist? Why or why not?*
3. *Were you already familiar with the term, "prevenient grace"? Why or why not? Where do you most experience prevenient grace in your life?*
4. *Can you identify with Kristina's story about her church experience? Why or why not? Have you ever felt out of place in a particular religious setting because you didn't speak the right lingo or act a certain way?*
5. *Can you think of stories or passages from scripture or experiences from your own life that either convey or call into question that God has an open-door policy?*

13

> **He Who Dies with The Most Toys Wins**
>
> **She Who Dies with The Most Toys Wins**

The thief comes only to steal and kill and destroy. I came that they may have life, and have it abundantly.
—Jesus (John 10:10)

Acquisition means life to miserable mortals.
—Hesiod

He/She Who Dies with The Most Toys Wins

SOME TIME AGO I saw a chilling picture in the newspaper *The Sun*.[1] The photo showed a newborn antelope snuggling up next to, of all things, a leopard. The scene might almost have passed for a Hallmark card, were it not for the fact that the picture only told part of the story.

What the picture didn't show was what the leopard would soon do when it got hungry, which is what leopards in the wild typically do when they get hungry. The caption underneath told the rest of the story: in a short while, the leopard would eat its newfound playmate for lunch. Still, for almost a whole hour before its ensuing kill, the leopard let this poor, helpless animal snuggle up next to it and even play with it, like a baby with its mother. The baby, oblivious to the danger it was in, had not been able to recognize its mother's cry and would die because of it. Nature in turn would take its cruel course.

There are reasons for the clichés, "every man for himself," "it's a jungle out there," and "it's a dog-eat-dog world." Darwin's principle, "survival of the fittest," is more than just a scientific theory with its adherents and detractors. I bet it plays out just about anywhere that human beings find themselves—on factory floors, in school classrooms, at recess time, and within our halls of government, not to mention in the church. Let's face it: the one with the most toys really does win much of the time. The more money, the more perks, the more physical advantages we are born with, and the more power we attain, the better off we tend to be in this world.

In this sense, materialism is at heart a very accurate statement about the nature of the universe. We inhabit bodies in a physical world that operates according to laws of nature in which there are predators and prey; the latest discoveries in science increasingly tell us that we are inevitably the sum of our genetic parts; and we are more and more conscious that we are what we consume.

But are we really *only* the sum of our material possessions? Is winning really nothing more than getting ahead of the pack, in

---

1. Mohan, "Moment a baby antelope walks into the jaws of a hungry leopard," para. 1–3.

The Life

terms of money, power, or success? Can life be reduced to merely learning how to survive in the face of Mother Nature's bleak arithmetic?

LISTENING FOR THE SHEPHERD'S VOICE

These days we hear a lot of voices that tell us what we should be. Fit, toned, rich, and beautiful, thanks to a gym membership and a secure retirement savings account or the latest in plastic surgery. Fashionable. Successful. Strong. Youthful.

Other times these voices only echo what we are hearing on the inside. The voices say, "I have to have more of (fill in the blank) to be somebody, to make my mark in this world, to survive and to win." They say, "I have to have more financial security," or "I've got to look more attractive," or, "I need more clout."

I can't even go shopping these days without having to hear the competing voices telling me who I am. Maybe you can identify. The other day I stepped into a store to buy a simple pair of jeans, only to be confronted by an overwhelming display of choices. There were

Rock star jeans.

Skinny boyfriend jeans.

Diva jeans.

Flirt jeans, or (if I didn't want to flirt), Sweetheart jeans.

Straight-leg, real jeans, as if to imply that the other jeans were somehow fake.

And then my favorite: Dreamer jeans.

I could choose any of these pairs in almost whatever style and pattern I preferred, from mid-rise or boot-cut to skinny or cropped, from the standard denim blue to yellow or polka-dotted.

I just wanted a pair of jeans—not an existential crisis!

This world's many voices compete for our attention in all sorts of ways, telling us we are what we buy, consume, wear, or play with. But the Bible says that when we listen to these voices too much and let them tell us who we are, we rob ourselves of the fullness of life God promises. And scripture has a funny way of telling us this. When the Bible conscripts imagery from the animal kingdom, it tends to land on less-than-flattering portrayals of human beings. A favorite comparison? Sheep. These annoyingly stupid, pathetically harmless, bleating yet endearing creatures are our closest equivalent. Why? Because when it comes to figuring out how to live well, we can be a lot like dumb sheep that go astray.

And Jesus, whom scripture describes as "the Good Shepherd," protects and sustains our lives.[2] He dutifully, faithfully, and lovingly leads the sheep (the ones who hear his voice, that is) from the safety of their pen to the rest and nourishment of green pastures and then back again. He guards the sheeps' comings and goings, protecting them from the wolves and thieves who would seek to steal, kill, and destroy.

This Jesus is the same anointed king of Israel of whom the Old Testament prophets speak. In a world in which the powerful prey on the weak and the rich on the poor, Jesus is the one, true, and trustworthy Shepherd. Jesus's is the one, often lonely voice telling us we're more than simply competitors in a Darwinian race to an ever-receding finish line—and Jesus stakes his life on it.

Here are the words of this Divine Shepherd as the prophet Ezekiel records them:

> I myself will search for my sheep, and will seek them out. I will bring them out from the peoples and gather them from the countries, and will bring them into their own land.... I will feed them with good pasture, and the mountain heights of Israel shall be their pasture; there they shall lie down in good grazing land, and they shall feed on rich pasture.... I will seek the lost, and I will bring back the strayed, and I will bind up the injured, and I will strengthen the weak, but the fat and the strong I will destroy. I will feed them with justice.[3]

Rich pastures that feed us.
    Homecomings for the lost.
    Healing for the sick.
    Strength for the weak.

2. John 10:11.
3. Ezekiel 34:11–19.

The Life

When God speaks, God's voice alters our materialistic reality: it points us in the direction of abundant life that far exceeds our dispirited modes of living and reveals our materialism for what it is—a spiritual stranglehold that can gradually squeeze the life right out of us.

Conversely, when we do not hear Jesus's voice, we are on our way to becoming dead sheep: it will be just a matter of time before the proverbial wolf, thief, or leopard snatches us away, before the other voices that tell us we're only material boys and girls will have their way with us in our undoing.[4]

There was a time when I used to worry about whether I was one of Jesus's sheep—whether I belonged to his fold. I don't anymore. That is because as I grapple with the words of the Good Shepherd in John 10, I am struck again by the nature of Jesus's mission: "I came that they [the sheep] may have life, and have it abundantly."[5]

The point is that we have life abundantly. Life that rings with a God-breathed purpose and dwells in God's love. Life that honors God's justice and will often demand some level of dying on our parts, but life that also does not run out and keeps bearing fruit even beyond the grave.

So maybe the more important question to contend with is not whether or not we can be sure we are "in," as those among Jesus's sheep. The question is really whether we are on the pathway to everlasting life, or whether we, like sheep gone astray, are just wandering off a cliff or into the waiting clutches of a wolf. The real issue is whether we are embracing life to the fullest.

Fullness of life, starting now, is why Jesus came, he says. It is also what you and I most want, I suspect, when we're most honest with ourselves. No toy, no matter the price, no matter the effectiveness of the advertising, can give me that. Besides, if I have to be a dumb sheep, I might as well be one with hope and a future.

---

4. Jesus says, "My sheep hear my voice." See John 10:27.
5. The brackets here are mine.

DISCUSSION QUESTIONS

1. Do you agree with Kristina's observation that "the one with the most toys wins" is an accurate description of our materialistic culture? Why or why not?
2. How does this materialistic reality contrast with the picture that Ezekiel paints of God's economy of justice (Ezekiel 34:11–19)?
3. What messages from our materialistic culture do you personally find hardest to drown out?
4. What are some characteristics of the abundant life to which God calls us?
5. When have you felt most alive in your life? Where were you? What were you doing?
6. How does it feel to be compared to a dumb, bleating sheep? How, if at all, do you relate to Jesus as the Good Shepherd? Has there been a time in your life when you knew it was Jesus shepherding you?

14

Well behaved women seldom make history.

The only people for me are the mad ones, the ones who are mad to live, mad to talk, mad to be saved, desirous of everything at the same time, the ones who never yawn or say a commonplace thing, but burn, burn, burn like fabulous yellow roman candles exploding like spiders across the stars.

—"Sal" in Jack Kerouac

Question authority.

—Another bumper sticker I see in my neighborhood

Growing up in evangelical Christian circles meant that sometime between losing my braces at fifteen and embarking on a seminary education, I internalized an implicit message that well-behaved women don't question authority, they simply follow it. Looking pretty, not asking too many questions, and certainly never challenging the prevailing authorities, even if they were misguided or corrupt—these were the prescribed duties that went along with being a woman in the church. Most diabolical of all was the insinuation that this was our duty because of divine and/or biblical authority.

Seminary, ordination, and ministry shone a light on the ways that these assumptions could not ultimately bear the test of lived experience. In a world in which authority, both within the church and outside it, is often exploitative, corrupt or misused, unquestioning obedience will eventually cause the most well-behaved women among us to lose our very selves.

This realization marked the beginning of my feminist awakening. It is also why I may one day have the courage to affix to my future Harley-Davidson the following bumper sticker: "Well-behaved women seldom make history." Because scripture is replete with examples of women who by the standards of their time behaved badly, but who, in choosing to question various societal norms, found meaning and significance and preserved and enriched their own lives and the lives of their neighbors.

Take the widow Ruth, for example. Her stubborn loyalty to her mother-in-law, Naomi, often earns her high marks as the good and dutiful daughter-in-law, but what about the bold seduction with which Ruth demonstrates this loyalty? In an effort to secure the continuation of her family's line, Ruth goes at night to her closest of kin, Boaz, "on the threshing floor" (an innuendo commonly associated with extramarital activity).[1] There Ruth lies down at Boaz's feet and tells him to cover her with his cloak (a euphemism for sexual relations). "Sin boldly," as the Protestant Reformer, Martin Luther once put it, might better sum up the mantra of this woman more often praised for her good behavior than for her attempted extramarital sexcapade with a man she hardly knew; it also lands Ruth in a continuing line of descendants that includes Jesus himself.[2]

---

1. See Hosea 9:1.
2. Luther, "Let Your Sins Be Strong," para. 14.

Or, take Rachel: no wallflower here.³ Best-selling author Rachel Held-Evans describes her namesake as follows:

> [Rachel is] a woman so captivating her husband pledged seven years of service in exchange for her hand, a woman whose determination to bear children sent her digging for mandrakes and bargaining with God, a woman brazen enough to steal her father's idols and hide them in a camel saddle, a woman who took her last breath on the side of the road, giving birth, a woman whose tomb survived obscurity, conquest, earthquakes, and riots to become one of the most venerated and contested sites of the Holy Land.⁴

There is Rahab, the prostitute, who at the risk of being labeled a traitor, aids and abets the mission of Israelite spies seeking to overthrow her city of Jericho.⁵ Her memorable act of treason hardly classifies as unquestioning obedience to authority or demure female behavior, but it does secure her and her family's own survival and even honor in the annals of God's chosen people.

And then there is Queen Esther. If sitting pretty on her divan eating bon bons were her trademark signature, she would never have risked her own head or the comforts of royalty on behalf of her people.

Mary, the mother of Jesus, is an unwed teenager when she learns that she will give birth to the Son of God; and the song she sings in praise of this very same God is deeply subversive. This God is one who "has brought down the powerful from their thrones and lifted up the lowly."⁶

Mary precedes a host of women in the New Testament who in their pursuit of Jesus are hardly rule keepers. The woman who scandalizes her contemporaries when she anoints Jesus's feet with alabaster perfume is one poignant example. Of her, Jesus says,

---

3. Genesis 31:19.
4. Held-Evans, *A Year of Biblical Womanhood*, 61.
5. Joshua 2.
6. Luke 1:52.

"Wherever the gospel is preached throughout the whole world, what she has done will also be told, in memory of her."[7]

But there are others: Mary, the sister of Martha, who eschews prevailing cultural expectations to study at the feet of Jesus; the Gentile woman who dares to approach Jesus and then directs a witty comeback at him after he insults her, with the result that she is the only person recorded in the New Testament to have changed God's mind; the Samaritan woman at the well whose life of promiscuity becomes fodder for personal testimony in the light of an encounter with Christ.[8]

I could go on.

These women remind me that pursuing Jesus is really not ultimately about being a good girl or doing the right thing or acting nice. These women invite me to ask instead whether I want to be truly *alive*. Sitting at Jesus' feet . . . surrendering to God's purposes for one's life . . . loving one's neighbor in radical, self-sacrificial ways . . . yes, even sinning boldly when one's survival, or the livelihood of others, bids it . . . such responses to a God who is Life Itself do not neatly equate with good behavior, because the equation itself is bogus, because Jesus himself is hardly boring or domesticated, nice or well-behaved according to prevailing social standards.

Dorothy Sayers puts it well:

> The people who hanged Christ never, to do them justice, accused Him of being a bore; on the contrary, they thought Him too dynamic to be safe. It has been left for later generations to muffle up that shattering personality and surround Him with an atmosphere of tedium. We have very efficiently pared the claws of the Lion of Judah, certified Him "meek and mild," and recommended Him as a fitting household pet for pale curates and pious old ladies.
>
> To those who knew Him, however, He in no way suggested a milk-and-water person; they objected to Him as a dangerous firebrand. True, he was tender to the unfortunate, patient with honest inquirers, and humble

---

7. Matthew 26.
8. Luke 10:39; Matthew 15:21–28; John 4.

before Heaven; but He insulted respectable clergymen by calling them hypocrites, He referred to King Herod as "that fox"; He went to parties in disreputable company and was looked upon as a "gluttonous man and a winebibber, a friend of publicans and sinners"; He assaulted indignant tradesmen and threw them and their belongings out of the Temple; He drove a coach-and-horses through a number of sacrosanct and hoary regulations; He cured diseases by any means that came handy, with a shocking casualness in the matter of other people's pigs and property; He showed no proper deference for wealth or social position.[9]

In the light of this vision of Jesus, even our worst deeds and our most shameful secrets become simply irrelevant. If they matter at all, they only matter to the degree that they have been swept up into the Life and have there been purified and emblazoned by the seal of this awe-inspiring "Lion of Judah." Otherwise, these things really are like chaff that the wind blows away.[10]

Where the Life is . . . is where our most memorable stories will be told . . . where the thrill of adventure wins out over fears of the unknown, and a traveler's wanderlust over concerns about comfort or self-preservation . . . where the magic of discovery bubbles over from within the hidden springs of the soul . . . where the very best things of this world, from music, art, the beauty of creation and a diversity of cultures, find their place not apart from but within this Life, pulsating with its rhythms, beating with its heart.

The Life is where the party is when you and I stumble back as prodigal sons and daughters to a God who saw us coming from a long way off and marks our return with a great celebration. The Life is that happening 80s dance party at a club where Jesus is the bouncer—and if you were wondering, Jesus has remarkably low standards for admission.[11] Just consider, for one thing, whom he

9. Sayers, *Creed or Chaos?*, 6–7, quoted in Marshall with Gilbert, *Heaven Is Not My Home*, 10–11.

10. Psalm 1.

11. This imagery borrows from and expands on a post I wrote for my blog, "Fellowship of Saints and Sinners," and has been republished with the permission of *Beliefnet*. See Kristina Robb-Dover, "Clubbing With Jesus," Fellowship

chooses to follow him: Judas, who probably carries a license with the word "Traitor" underneath his name, and is stealing drinks from the bar; Peter, who could turn violent at the drop of a hat; Mary Magdalene, who, if legend is correct, probably knows at least the ancient equivalent of pole dancing; the Apostle Paul, who might be yelling racist slurs and throwing F-bombs.

If it's true that "anyone who calls upon the name of the Lord [Jesus] will be saved," as scripture claims, then Jesus will be letting in a whole lot of people we won't want to be around.[12] They'll be there on the dance floor under the strobe lights grooving to the beat. And, I can't help but laugh when I think about what that picture might look like some day: Pat Robertson doing the *macarena* with Barack Obama; James Dobson surrounded by not one but two lesbians moving to the beat of "Dancing Queen" while playing with his tie; maybe even an avowed atheist like Christopher Hitchens getting down with Billy Graham.

You and I might be there, too, surrounded by all those we would most prefer not to see.

That is because the Life is where the main plot happens, where God is doing "God things" that involve you and me as often unsuspecting players in a big Story that, as Rob Bell puts it, is about the "whole universe being brought back into harmony with its Maker."[13]

The Life is where you really will feel most alive.

The Life animates and reanimates every one of our stories worth telling and retelling, in the very same breath that it reminds us that those stories are not ultimately about us, or about our own best behavior.

The Life—not your greatest achievements, worst shortcomings or biggest failures—can make your own life worth remembering, celebrating, and living passionately, too.

---

of Saints and Sinners, *Beliefnet*.

12. Romans 10:13.
13. Bell, *Velvet Elvis*, 109.

The Life

DISCUSSION QUESTIONS

1. Do you agree or disagree with this bumper sticker, and why?
2. Can you think of a well-behaved woman in Scripture or history whom you admire? Why or why not?
3. What constitutes a memorable life story for you and why?
4. When were you on your worst behavior? How, if at all, was the experience life-giving for you?
5. Where do you catch glimmers of the Life in your own life? When have you felt you had a part in a God story? What, if anything, did the experience teach you about how you would like to be remembered?

15

God Wants Spiritual Fruit, Not Religious Nuts

Well, some nuts are fruits and some are seeds. I'm sure there is something in the seed part. Also nut allergies seem to be on the rise. Smirk.

—Facebook friend Kate Nase McLean, reacting to this bumper sticker

But the fruit of the Spirit is love, joy, peace, patience, kindness, generosity, faithfulness, gentleness and self-control. Against such things there is no law. Those who belong to Christ Jesus have crucified the flesh with its passions and desires. If we live by the Spirit, let us also be guided by the Spirit.

—Galatians 5:22–23

The Life

One Lent I decided that instead of abstaining from sweets, swearing, or other vices I am prone to, I would try to cultivate a spiritual fruit instead. I chose patience. Someone in the congregation I was serving at the time decided I could use a little help: she showed up in my office one day with a wrist band that spelled in little plastic beads, "P-A-T-I-E-N-C-E."

I gratefully wore that bracelet throughout Lent as a reminder of my need for the Holy Spirit. At frustratingly long traffic lights. In achingly dull church committee meetings. With slightly annoying people of the kind who inspired the 1968 John Cleese film, *How To Irritate People*.[1] That little bauble was there to remind me of the new and improved, more patient me I was becoming, thanks to the work of the Spirit; and, I wore it with penitent expectation that God would transform chronic impatience into steadfast, longsuffering fortitude.

The scheme worked . . . for a time. Then at some point in the days after Lent that bracelet went missing—maybe at the gym or at the bottom of my daughter's toy chest—and I found it easy to return to old patterns. (I guess self-discipline has never really been my forté, either. Maybe I'll work on that next year.)

It would seem that bearing spiritual fruit and living the kind of Spirit-filled, abundant life Jesus invites us to embrace really do not come naturally, at least for most of us. Becoming a "religious nut" is probably easier—and for this reason probably more common. You don't have to look too far to find obnoxious displays of religious legalism, bigotry, and intolerance—or worse, weird cults and suicide bombers. But persons whose lives overflow with gifts like love and joy, peace and gentleness . . . even when they're in the shower with nobody around . . . and there is no hot water? Even when they're not in church? I bet you can count the ones you know on one hand.

---

1. The 1968 television broadcast, *How To Irritate People*, written by John Cleese, Graham Chapman, Marty Feldman, and Tim Brooke-Taylor, features various sketches illustrating ways to be irritating. My favorite of these is one in which a bored pilot on a commercial airline begins to broadcast intercom messages to passengers, reassuring them that they have nothing to worry about (with the result that the passengers inevitably become worried).

These few are also generally the ones who have moved from marketing Jesus to actually following him. Imperfectly, sure, but consistently, with the kind of attachment that really bears fruit, fruit of the spiritual variety.

"I know it when I see it," a justice of the Supreme Court once said of obscenity in a landmark ruling.[2]

We tend to know spiritual fruit when we see it.

Spiritual fruit grows on people who abide in Jesus. People of this sort are like trees "planted by streams of water, which yield their fruit in its season," whose "leaves do not wither."[3] They prosper—not because they have fame or fortune or a killer bod or faultless morals—but because they reflect God's self-giving love, the best, clearest demonstration of which is Jesus on a cross.

These are the people who have let Jesus lead them where he wants to take them—even when that means going to the cross and "dying" to old ways, often over and over again. And it is this dying part I find most difficult. Usually when I think of crucifixion, I conceive of lots of pain and gore—you know, a long, Shakespearean death, like the expiration of Hamlet only ten times worse—and honestly, who wants all that gruesomeness? There is something reassuring about staying unchanged, forever.

Barren, okay.

Adolescent, yes.

Yet forever young. Forever untouched by the wintry season of heartbreak and loss.

But bearing spiritual fruit requires letting our lives be grafted into the Vine that is Jesus, so that our lives more intentionally reflect and exude the life of Christ (the Life). This process demands some level of dying to those past ways of living and self-destructive behaviors that would rob us of the fullness of life God offers. Love, joy, peace, patience, kindness, generosity, faithfulness, gentleness,

---

2. The phrase, "I know it when I see it," first coined by Justice Potter Stewart to define obscenity in the 1964 case, Jacobellis v. Ohio, "became one of the most famous in the history of the Supreme Court," according to *Wikipedia*, s.v. "I know it when I see it," http//en.wikipedia.org/wiki/I_know_it_when_I_see_it. (accessed September 25, 2013).

3. Psalm 1:3.

and self-control? These all belong to the same tree or vine that is Jesus. They are all outgrowths of a painful but life-giving transplant.

And the Holy Spirit is the fertilizer.

On most days I find I need a serious dose of that Miracle Gro. Only on some days do I remember to ask God for it. But when I do, I find I'm better able to see that fruit in myself, in others, and in God's creation. The gentleness of my husband's touch. The generosity of a neighbor. The kindness of a young child sharing her lunch with a friend. The joy of new beginnings in the rising of the sun, like laughter breaking out across the face of a God who smiles upon us.

When viewed in the light of the Holy Spirit, the color and dimensions of my world take on a new clarity and depth. The experience is a bit like watching high-definition television on a flat-screen TV. after trading in that old, wood-paneled clunker that only shows programs in black and white. In this way, the Holy Spirit also functions as corrective lenses: She helps us see—*really* see, maybe for the first time—all that surrounds us in a clearer, brighter, more vivid quality.[4]

So there is both a challenge and a promise in Jesus's command to abide in him like branches on a tree. "Remain in me, and I will remain in you," Jesus says.

"Belong to me," in other words.

"Stick close to me."

"Put your roots in me."

"Drink from me."

"Live in me."

The spiritual fruit will come in due season, leaving us painfully changed, yes, but for the better—more like we were meant to be from the very beginning, more plentifully alive as God would have us live.

"We know what we are, but not what we may be," Shakespeare writes, but I wonder if we really do know what we are.[5] Do we know that as human beings we are mere dust wonderfully formed by the very breath of God and made in God's image? Do we know

---

4. "Holy Spirit" in Hebrew is the feminine noun *ruach*.

5. Shakespeare, "Hamlet," *The Complete Works of William Shakespeare*, 4:5, 1100.

that this same breath that animated the first man and woman and now enlivens our own bodies, can also fashion our ongoing transformation? Do we know that because of this very same Spirit, our lives have the capacity to be caught up in, and reshaped and reinvigorated by the very life of God?

Knowing what we are hints at what we may be; but it also reminds us to whom we really belong—and we belong to God. We, like all creation, belong to the Life. The dynamic, electrifying movement of God can pulse in our lives, too, so that our hearts move to the beat of a divine disc jockey rather than those old, boring and lifeless rhythms we have become accustomed to.

Henri Nouwen describes this Spirit-led transformation of those who belong to Christ with four words: "taken, blessed, broken, and given."[6] We are "taken" insofar as we have been created by God from the very beginning as special, unique, and beautiful, just like every other person in this world. We are also "blessed" with the very presence and power of God's love for us, a presence and power that both blesses us and calls us to bless others. We are "broken": nobody else, Nouwen writes, knows your own unique pain, excepting God Himself; but this suffering, when "put under the blessing of God," can be a gift. We are taken, blessed and broken in order to be "given" to the world.

Bread for the world. Like the body and blood of our Lord Jesus Christ, given for you and for me. Love, joy, peace, patience, kindness, generosity, faithfulness, gentleness, and self-control are what it looks like to be "taken, blessed, broken, and given" to the world. These gifts are the outward signs of an inward grace with which we might serve one another and our world, all because the Spirit feeds us.

YOUR INVITATION

There is an ancient Chinese parable about an old man who before he died wanted to know what heaven and hell were like and sought the advice of a wise man in his village. The wise man led him down

---

6. Nouwen, *Life of the Beloved*, 43–84.

a path to a large house with many rooms. There they found lots of people around a great, big banquet table, each of them holding twelve-foot-long chopsticks and looking emaciated.

"Now I know what hell looks like," the old man said. "Will you please show me what heaven looks like?"

The wise man took him down the same path just a little further until they came upon another large house much like the first, also with many people inside, all of them also at a lavish banquet table, each of them also with a pair of twelve-foot-long chopsticks. This time, though, the people looked well-fed and content.

This puzzled the old man, who asked for an explanation.

"In heaven we feed each other," the wise man replied.

When we belong to Jesus, we feed each other. We become guests at God's table and join in the life of God's party. Fortunately, the one who invites us to the party also leads us there, to a place right at the Host's table and to a big, steaming dish of hot food and the company of dear friends, all feeding one another.

There we'll be: the poor, the crippled, the lame, and the blind, stuffing one another's faces with the best-tasting feast we've ever had at a party that never grows old.

We never have to doubt that we belong there, because each of us has an invitation with our name on it in gold lettering.

DISCUSSION QUESTIONS

1. *Have you ever met a "religious nut"? What, in your opinion, distinguishes a religious nut from someone with spiritual fruit?*

2. *Who in your own life most displays the fruit of the Spirit, and how?*

3. *What one spiritual fruit do you either most admire or most lack (or both)?*

4. *Do you have the assurance that you belong to God? If so, how has that awareness changed you? How has it changed your relationships with others? Alternatively, if you don't have the assurance that you belong to God, to what are you belonging more*

these days?

5. *How does Kristina's imagery of the Holy Spirit as "fertilizer" or "corrective lenses" resonate with you? Does it in any way describe your own experience? Why or why not?*

6. *What in you may need to die in order for you to become that beloved person God says you are? How might you entrust yourself to the Spirit's leading to take you there?*

7. *What most intimidates you about living a life in the Spirit?*

8. *How does the imagery of a great banquet and many undeserving guests feeding each other resonate with you? Does it inspire you or scare you, or both? Is it a helpful way to think about the nature of spiritual fruit like love, joy, peace, patience, kindness, generosity, faithfulness, gentleness, and self-control?*

16

got hope?

In my end is my beginning.
—T.S. Eliot

Hold me fast, hold me fast, cuz I'm a hopeless wanderer.
—Mumford & Sons

By [God's] great mercy, God has given us a new birth into a living hope through the resurrection of Jesus Christ from the dead.
—1 Peter 1:3

got hope?

I KNOW WHAT'S IT'S LIKE to feel hopeless.

Hopelessness can seem as suffocating as being stuck in a small, cramped room with no windows; if there is light outside, you can't see it; and that locked door won't open from the inside. Someone else on the outside has to open the door for you.

When you stop hoping, breath itself can seem a burden—and, in this sense, I have reason to believe that hope really is a matter of life or death.

Hope. An implicit trust that the future promises better. An expectancy that where there is death, new life is just around the corner—that, like a phoenix, fresh beginnings arise from the ashes of our endings.

Hope is what makes Christians "eternal beginners."[1]

The contemporary German theologian, Jürgen Moltmann, who has written often about hope since his conversion to Christianity in a prisoner of war camp during World War II, defines hope as "the power of resurrection from life's failures and defeats."[2] And, the promise in scripture is clear: because Jesus rose from the dead, we, too, have access to that "power of resurrection." The resurrection of Jesus is the basis for hoping in even the worst of situations: it is why small shafts of light can come streaming through even our darkest rooms of despair. Hope is grounded in the ongoing power of Christ's resurrection to make a way where there is none—to forge new beginnings out of all our endings, however final they might seem.

The uniqueness of Christianity resides in this hope. "Nowhere else in the world of the religions is God associated with human hope for the future," Moltmann writes.[3] "Christianity is wholly and entirely confident hope, a stretching out to what is ahead, and a readiness for a fresh start."[4]

And, if it is true that the absence of hope "plunges us into despair," as the third-century theologian John Chrysostom once put it,

---

1. Franz Rosenzweig, quoted by Jürgen Moltmann in *In the End—The Beginning*, xi.
2. Ibid., ix.
3. Ibid., 87.
4. Ibid.

The Life

it is also true, according to Moltmann, that "all despair presupposes hope."[5] "The pain of despair lies in the fact that a hope is there, but no way opens up towards its fulfillment," Moltmann writes.[6] Even despair itself presumes the existence of hope.

THE CLOSED DOOR

The Bible is full of people entitled to despair.[7] One of them is Martha, the sister of Lazarus, in the wake of her brother's death. When Jesus finally arrives to console her, Lazarus has already been dead four days—and this in spite of Martha's best efforts to send for her friend Jesus when Lazarus might still have been healed.

When we meet Martha in John 11, she and her sister Mary are going through all the customary stages of grief. The burial on the day of death. The long procession to the tomb. An even longer procession of empty-sounding words—all those well-meaning expressions of sympathy that can ring hollow in the immediate aftermath of great loss.

"I'm so sorry for your loss."
"Let us know if there's anything we can do."
"He's no longer in pain."
"He knew the Lord."
"He's in a better place now."

Can you picture yourself for a moment in Martha's shoes? Tearful hugs and empty Kleenex boxes. Flowers and more flowers on the kitchen table. Hordes of family you haven't seen in ages, including crazy old Aunt Ethel. The last time you saw her she was stuffing her purse with a portion of meatloaf and cornbread from the buffet at Golden Corral.

But, *oh no!*, that reminds you—because when you're Martha you're always thinking of what needs to be done—*there is still the*

---

5. Ibid., 93.

6. Moltmann, *Theology of Hope*, 23.

7. The rest of this chapter borrows heavily from one of my sermons and is here reprinted with the permission of *Beliefnet*. See Kristina Robb-Dover, "The Resurrection and the Life: A Sermon," Fellowship of Saints and Sinners.

reception for the memorial service to worry about and the caterer to call and the menu to review.

Mini pigs in a blanket? Probably not.

Artichoke and goat cheese crudité or tomato bruschetta? Maybe . . . But, I don't know. Do I have a choice? you wonder. *What else is on offer?*

What about a world in which loved ones don't get sick and die?

What about a world in which God actually lives up to God's side of the bargain?

What about a world in which a dear friend like Jesus who is supposed to be the Messiah, the very Son of God, shows up when it matters—when something could have still been done, when healing and recovery weren't so out-of-this-world impossible?

Martha would rather have ordered that instead. In fact she has already tried. Four days ago when Lazarus was in a bad way but still alive, Martha had sent for Jesus. She had cried out to God for her brother's deliverance.

But God hadn't come. God hadn't even replied to say God had other, bigger, more pressing things to attend to, like ending wars or bringing justice to the oppressed. The promises of the prophet Isaiah—promises of a new heaven and earth in which weeping will cease, in which the labor of our hands is not in vain, in which bad things don't happen to good people?[8] All this was supposed to be on the menu, or so Martha had thought, because God loved her, because she and God had been extra chummy, because God in Jesus was doing a new thing for this broken world full of broken people.

But now Martha is instead choosing finger foods for her brother's memorial service. "If only God had shown up in time," she's saying, like everybody else who knew and loved Lazarus.

And when Jesus finally does show up on the scene, when he comes to Martha and says, "Your brother will rise again," Jesus's arrival seems too little, too late.

And maybe Martha can be forgiven for dismissing Jesus's words to her as yet another empty expression of sympathy, akin to "your brother's in a better place now." Because Martha, like most

---

8. Isaiah 65.

The Life

Jews in her time, and maybe like many of us, is accustomed to believing in some distant future resurrection. She probably knows all the religious code language by heart. Those of us who recite the words of the Apostles' Creed every Sunday in church can perhaps identify: "I believe in Jesus Christ, his only Son, our Lord . . . I believe in the Holy Spirit, the holy catholic church, the communion of saints, the forgiveness of sins, the resurrection of the body and life everlasting," we say, affirming by rote the basic tenets of our faith.

"Resurrection," for Martha, probably belongs to a well rehearsed religious vocabulary, one that offers only shallow comfort in the face of her present loss; and when you're standing knee-deep in tragedy, resurrection can sound like just another hollow-sounding religious gimmick, maybe of the kind we sometimes see on TV: the televangelist stares into the camera promising healing or prosperity to the next caller with a credit card; and, we would like to believe, but we know better.

Resurrection from the dead? Who really buys that claptrap in the twenty-first century? we may wonder if not speak aloud.

THE OPEN DOOR

Not long ago I happened by the Macy's Estee Lauder cosmetics counter. The sales lady, in addition to insisting that I sit for a full make-over, was all the while singing the praises of the latest in Estee Lauder skin products. Estee Lauder's nightly repair serum had done wonders for her skin and would for mine. Those under-eye wrinkles? Those stress lines? Those sun spots? They didn't have to be the final story. With Estee Lauder's nightly repair serum, I would be resurrected to a more youthful looking version of myself. And if you have to know, she convinced me. Resurrection was standing right in front of me in the shape of a ridiculously expensive, one-ounce bottle, and I believed her.

But when resurrection is standing right in front of you in the form of a person, a person who says, "I am the Resurrection and the Life," a person who has healed all sorts of strangers but then failed to show up for his own friends—you and your brother, Lazarus—you might not be such a sucker.

Because we, like Martha, catch on pretty quickly that life manages to go on in the face of death. Often mind-numbingly so. Often without rhyme or reason. If it's not the loss of a dear friend or family member, there are all those mini deaths to contend with.

The child we once thought had a bright future struck down by a life-threatening addiction.

The relationship we once believed to be a storybook romance now in pieces.

The lay-off from a job we thought we were to retire in.

The untimely diagnosis of cancer.

We all have our often hidden griefs to bear—those things that over time we have learned to hold quietly to ourselves. It's hard to imagine resurrection in these places where we find ourselves saying with Martha, "If only, God."

But some of us also know the end of this story. If Martha has reason to doubt that Jesus signifies new life in the immediate moment, the kind of spiritual rebirth that defies even death itself and will one day be embodied in a new, perfected, physical body for ourselves and for all creation, then in just a little while Martha will be obliged to change her mind.

First she'll watch Jesus become so greatly troubled—"angered" the original Greek implies—by a world in which people have to die. Then she'll watch as Jesus in the presence of many onlookers commands Lazarus to come out of his tomb. And then the most mind-blowing, earth-shattering thing of all will happen: she'll watch as Lazarus obeys Jesus and does in fact stumble out, as if waking from a long sleep, rubbing his eyes while accustoming himself to the light, his burial garments still clinging to his skin.

And then and there Martha will see that there really *is* reason to believe that in Jesus are fulfilled all the promises of old of the prophet Isaiah. Promises of a new heaven and a new earth. Promises of a dwelling place where weeping and suffering and death are no more, where all is put right with our broken world.

Because when Jesus says he is the Resurrection and the Life, He is saying that God's very nature is one of second chances. He is saying that the new life God offers is as dependable as the dawning of each new day. And, these little spiritual rebirths are but a foretaste of a day when in God's perfect timing the dead shall rise, when all of our paths shall be made straight, and when God's seal of grace will finally and decisively set itself upon our wayward hearts, like a lover with his long-awaited beloved. In that day, all humankind will see "the glory of the Lord," in the words of the prophet Isaiah, this "glory" being the restoration of all creation under God's perfect reign.[9]

Hope in this context is little more than a surrendering to God's economy of grace: it is releasing our expectations for how God should work, because resurrection never happens apart from God's timing and on God's own terms. And God's timing and God's terms, as Martha will soon discover, don't abide by our I-must-have-it-now culture of instant gratification.

Frank Partnoy, a professor of law and finance at the University of San Diego School of Law, has written a book titled, *Wait: The Art and Science of Delay*, in which Partnoy makes the case that learning how to manage delay (learning how to wait, in other words) is one of life's most important lessons. People who can learn to wait for good things will be happier and more fulfilled, and will make better decisions, Partnoy believes.[10]

But I suspect many of us have wondered along with Martha why God procrastinates so much when it comes to our own agendas. *Why not now, God?*, we wonder, about our healing from a chronic illness or our deliverance from an addiction . . . about peace in the Middle East . . . about an end to hunger and poverty and injustice? *If you, God, really are who you say you are, if you really are "the Resurrection and the Life," why must we wait so long for you to burst onto the scene and fix things?*

Maybe we, like Martha, must discover why God's delayed ways are so far superior to our own hasty ones. Maybe we must simply trust in God's perfect timing. Because if resurrection is central to the character of God, it is also entirely an act of God for which we

---

9. Isaiah 40:5.
10. Partnoy, *Wait: The Art and Science of Delay*.

can only wait. We can look for that new life right around the bend; we can pray for it and work for it; we can surrender to it when it comes; but ultimately God alone is the source of that resurrection power which comprises our hope.

God alone can open the door to that small, cramped room with no windows and only a few shafts of light streaming through.

A friend of mine was a correction officer in a juvenile rehabilitation center in Kansas City, Missouri. I asked her what kept her going in an often discouraging job in one of our nation's most depressed regions. Kansas City apparently boasts one of the highest rates of inner-city violence in this country.

By way of example my friend shared a story of one boy who by the age of fourteen had spent years on the street as a hardened gang member. One day this boy, who according to my friend was not a small boy, became belligerent. My friend, seeking to restrain the boy, had grabbed him in an iron-tight hold. In those few, tense moments, as she stood there holding on to a kid whose life until now had been a series of dead ends, my friend's heart opened and her grip on the boy relaxed. There these two stood, locked in a great, big bear hug, my friend and this rough-and-tumble kid, who began to sob like a scared, little baby who just wanted to be held.

Resurrection.

Resurrection for Martha.

Resurrection for a no-nonsense correction officer and a hardened, under-age criminal. On God's terms. At God's time.

Resurrection for you and for me, too.

Thankfully, God's resurrection does not depend on our own, self-generated belief in order to be real.

"What is truly good in human life does not depend upon our capacity to manufacture it," it has been said.[11] The same could be said of resurrection. God's power to bring new life out of all our dead ends happens *in spite* of, not *because* of, our doings. Hope simply gives voice to that power—the power of the one who is himself the Resurrection and the Life.

---

11. Long, *The Witness of Preaching*, 6.

The Life

Hope has made its way back to me, and I to it. Maybe hope never left in fact. Maybe it was just waiting to be discovered beneath all those layers of false hopes—all those things I had thought, at least implicitly, were the ticket to a bright future.

Hope as the power of resurrection from life's failures and defeats. Hope that can fill you with all joy and peace in believing, and that by the power of the Holy Spirit may abound in your heart when everything else in this weary world very well may disappoint you.[12]

Hope that gives a reason to live—and to live abundantly.

Hope for living.

Living hope.

Got any?

DISCUSSION QUESTIONS

1. *What do you make of Moltmann's definition of hope as "the power of resurrection from life's failures and defeats"? How is such hope that which does not disappoint? Is it possible to talk of hope that really doesn't disappoint without talking about resurrection?*

2. *Is hope a scarce commodity in our society? In what ways have you hoped and then been disappointed?*

3. *Have you ever been hopeless? What was it like?*

4. *How have you experienced hope? In what way does your story compare with Kristina's or Martha's and/or other figures from scripture?*

5. *How might we tell a story that is more full of hope about ourselves and our world, one that does not disappoint?*

---

12. Romans 15:13.

Bibliography

Allen, Woody. *Woody Allen Standup Comic: 1964–1968*. Los Angeles: Rhino Records, 1999.
Balthasar, Hans Urs von. *Heart of the World*. Translated by Erasmo S. Leiva. San Francisco: Ignatius, 1954.
Barth, Karl. *Church Dogmatics*, III/4: *The Doctrine of Creation*. Edited by G. W. Bromiley and T. F. Torrance. Peabody, MA: Hendrickson, 2010.
———. *The Word in This World: Two Sermons*. Edited by Kurt I. Johansen and translated by Christopher Asprey. Vancouver, BC: Regent College Publishing, 2007.
Becker, Amy Julia. About Page, "Thin Places, *Patheos*. Online: http://www.patheos.com/blogs/thinplaces/about/.
———. "Blessed Imperfection," "Thin Places, *Patheos*. Online: http://www.patheos.com/blogs/thinplaces/2013/02/blessed-imperfection-a-girl-learns-to-jump-and-her-mother-to-take-her-first-steps-by-kristina-robb-dover/.
Bee, Samantha. *I Know I Am, But What Are You?* New York: Gallery, 2010.
Bell, Rob. *Love Wins*. New York: HarperCollins, 2011.
———. *Velvet Elvis: Repainting the Christian Faith*. New York: HarperCollins, 2005.
Berry, Wendell. "Manifesto: The Mad Farmer Liberation Front." *The Country of Marriage*. Berkeley, CA: Counterpoint, 1971.
Bono. "The Rolling Stone Interview: Bono." Interview by Jann Wenner. *The Rolling Stone*, November 3, 2005. Online: http://www.jannswenner.com/archives/Bono.aspx.
Campbell, Joseph. *Reflections on the Art of Living: A Joseph Campbell Companion*. Edited by Diane K. Osbon. New York: HarperCollins, 1991.
Cold Play. *Mylo Xyloto*. London: EMI, 2011.
Copeland, Adam. "No need for church: Ministry with young adults in flux." *The Christian Century*, January 24, 2012. Online: http://www.christiancentury.org/article/2012-01/no-need-church.
de Magdeburg, Mechtild. *The Flowing Light of the Godhead*. Mahwah, NJ: Paulist, 1998.

Dikkers, Scott, ed. *Our Dumb Century: 100 Years of Headlines from America's Finest News Source.* New York: Three Rivers, 1999.

The Economist Group. "Marcella Putyn." *The Economist*, April 27, 2013, 86.

Foster, Richard. *Celebration of Discipline*, 3rd ed. San Francisco: HarperSanFrancisco, 1978.

Eliot, T. S. "East Coker." *Four Quartets.* New York: Mariner Books, 1943.

Gardner, Carol. *Bumper Sticker Wisdom: America's Pulpit Above the Tailpipe.* Hillsboro, OR: Beyond Words, 1995.

Gregory of Nyssa. *The Life of Moses.* New York: HarperCollins, 1978.

Hadewijch of Antwerp. *Hadewijch: The Complete Works.* Translated by Mother Columba Hart. Mahwah, NJ: Paulist, 1980.

Held-Evans, Rachel. *A Year of Biblical Womanhood.* Nashville: Thomas Nelson, 2012.

Heschel, Abraham. *Man Is Not Alone: A Philosophy of Religion.* New York: Farrar, Straus and Giroux, 1951.

Hesiod. *Theogony.* Translated and introduced by Richard S. Caldwell. Newbury Port, MA: Focus Information Group, Inc., 1987.

Kaling, Mindy. *Is Everyone Hanging Out Without Me? (And Other Concerns).* New York: Three Rivers, 2011.

Kehe, Marjorie. "Anne Rice says she's done with Christianity." *The Christian Science Monitor*, July 30, 2010. Online: http://www.csmonitor.com/Books/chapter-and-verse/2010/0730/Anne-Rice-says-she-s-done-with-Christianity.

Kerouac, Jack. *On the Road.* New York: Penguin, 1959.

Kosmin, Barry A., et al. "American Nones: The Profile of the No Religion Population." Hartford, CT: Trinity College, 2008. Online: http://commons.trincoll.edu/aris/files/2011/08/NONES_08.pdf.

Labberton, Mark. *The Dangerous Act of Worship.* Downers Grove, IL: InterVarsity, 2007.

Lamott, Anne. *Bird by Bird: Some Instructions on Writing and Life.* New York: Anchor, 1994.

Lennon, John. *Double Fantasy.* New York: Geffen Records, 1980.

Lewis, C. S. *The Great Divorce.* San Francisco: HarperSanFrancisco, 1946.

———. *The Problem of Pain.* San Francisco: HarperSanFrancisco, 2001.

Long, Tom. *The Witness of Preaching*, 2nd ed. Louisville: Westminster John Knox, 2005.

Louis C. K. "Q&A: Louis CK on 'Louie,' lenses and knowing when you're lucky." Interview by Robert Lloyd. *Los Angeles Times*, July 7, 2011. Online: http://latimesblogs.latimes.com/showtracker/2011/07/qa-louis-ck.html.

Lugo, Luis, et al. "U.S. Religious Landscape Survey: Religious Affiliation: Diverse and Dynamic." Washington, DC: Pew Forum on Religion and Public Life, February 2008.

Luther, Martin. "Let Your Sins Be Strong: A Letter from Luther to Melanchthon." Translated by Erika Flores for Project Wittenberg. Online: http://www.scrollpublishing.com/store/Luther-Sin-Boldly.html.

Grace Sticks

Manning, Brennan. *All Is Grace*. Colorado Springs: David C. Cook, 2011.

Marshall, Paul, with Lela Gilbert. *Heaven Is Not My Home*. Nashville: Word, 1998.

Miller, Paul. *The Praying Life*. Colorado Springs: NavPress, 2009.

Mohan, Dominic. "Moment a baby antelope walks into the jaws of a hungry leopard." *The Sun*, April 19, 2012. Online: http://www.thesun.co.uk/sol/homepage/news/4262289/Baby-antelope-killed-by-leopard-it-was-playing-with-in-Sabi-Sand-Game-Reserve-in-South-Africa.html.

Moltmann, Jürgen. *In the End—The Beginning*. Minneapolis: Fortress, 2004.

———. *Theology of Hope*. Minneapolis: Fortress, 1993.

Mumford & Sons. *Babel*. New York: Glassnote Records, 2012.

Nouwen, Henri. *Life of the Beloved: Spiritual Living in a Secular World*. New York: Crossroad, 1992.

Palmer, Parker. *The Hidden Wholeness*. San Francisco: Jossey-Bass, 2004.

Parker, James. "Reliving Groundhog Day." *The Atlantic*, February 20, 2012. Online: http://www.theatlantic.com/magazine/archive/2013/03/reliving-groundhog-day/309223/.

———. "The Filthy Moralist: How the comedian Louis C. K. became America's unlikely conscience." *The Atlantic*, April 2, 2012. Online: http://www.theatlantic.com/magazine/archive/2012/05/the-filthy-moralist/308940/.

Partnoy, Frank. *Wait: The Art and Science of Delay*. *The Diane Rehm Show*. Interview by Diane Rehm. National Public Radio, July 10, 2012.

The Presbyterian Church (U.S.A.). *The Constitution of the Presbyterian Church, Part I: Book of Confessions*. Louisville: The Office of the General Assembly, 2004.

Robb-Dover, Kristina. Fellowship of Saints and Sinners. *Beliefnet*. No pages. Online: http://blog.beliefnet.com/fellowshipofsaintsandsinners/.

———. "Blessed Imperfection: A Girl Learns To Jump and Her Mother To Take Her First Steps." Thin Places. By Amy Julia Becker. *Patheos*. No pages. Online: http://www.patheos.com/blogs/thinplaces/2013/02/blessed-imperfection-a-girl-learns-to-jump-and-her-mother-to-take-her-first-steps-by-kristina-robb-dover/#disqus_thread.

Rohr, Richard. *Near Occasions of Grace*. New York: Orbis, 1993.

Sayers, Dorothy. *Creed or Chaos?* Manchester, NH: Sophia Institute, 1974.

Schmidt, Leigh Eric. *Restless Souls: The Making of American Spirituality*. New York: HarperCollins, 2005.

Shakespeare, William. *Hamlet*. In *The Complete Works of Shakespeare*. New York: Chatham River, 1975.

———. *The Tempest*. In *The Complete Works of Shakespeare*. New York: Chatham River Press, 1975.

Stencel, Sandra, et al. "'Nones' on the Rise: One-in-Five Adults Have No Religious Association." Washington, D.C.: Pew Forum on Religion and Public Life, 2012, 1–80. Online: http://www.pewforum.org/uploadedFiles/Topics/Religious_Affiliation/Unaffiliated/NonesOnTheRise-full.pdf.

Swoboda, A. J. *Messy: God Likes It That Way*. Grand Rapids: Kregel, 2012.

Taylor, Barbara Brown. *An Altar in the World: A Geography of Faith.* San Francisco: HarperOne, 2009.

Tennent, Tim. "Bumper Sticker Christianity." No pages. Online: http://timothytennent.com/2011/09/21/bumper-sticker-christianity/.

U2. *The Joshua Tree.* Dublin, Ireland: Danesmoate House, 1987.

Wilde, Oscar. *De Profundis.* Lenox, MA: Hard Press, 2006.

Yehoshua, A. B. "Boundaries and Crossing." Interview by Vered Shemtov (4 March 2004). *Sh'ma: A Journal of Jewish Ideas*, March 2004. No pages. Online: http://shma.com/2004/03/boundaries-and-crossing/.

Zierman, Addie. "Making Your Faith Your Own." *How To Talk Evangelical.* No pages. Online: http://howtotalkevangelical.addiezierman.com/?p=1582.

www.ingramcontent.com/pod-product-compliance
Lightning Source LLC
Chambersburg PA
CBHW020853160426
43192CB00007B/900